Career Launcher

Film

Career Launcher series

Advertising and Public Relations
Computers and Programming
Education
Energy
Fashion
Film
Finance
Food Services
Hospitality
Internet
Health Care Management
Health Care Providers
Law
Law Enforcement and Public Safety
Manufacturing
Nonprofit Organizations
Performing Arts
Professional Sports Organizations
Real Estate
Recording Industry
Television
Video Games

Career Launcher

Film

Candace S. Gulko

Ferguson Publishing
An imprint of Infobase Publishing

Career Launcher: **Film** FEB 0 2 2011

Ferguson
An imprint of Infobase Publishing
132 West 31st Street
New York NY 10001

Library of Congress Cataloging-in-Publication Data

Gulko, Candace S.
    Film / Candace S. Gulko ; foreword by Peter Haratonik.
        p. cm. — (Career launcher)
    Includes bibliographical references and index.
    ISBN-13: 978-0-8160-7959-9 (hardcover : alk. paper)
    ISBN-10: 0-8160-7959-5 (hardcover : alk. paper)
1. Motion pictures—Vocational guidance—Juvenile literature.
I. Title. II. Series.
    PN1995.9.P75G85 2010
    791.43023—dc22

                                                              2009051279

Ferguson books are available at special discounts when purchased in bulk quantities for businesses, associations, institutions, or sales promotions. Please call our Special Sales Department in New York at (212) 967-8800 or (800) 322-8755.

You can find Ferguson on the World Wide Web at http://www.fergpubco.com

Produced by Print Matters, Inc.
Text design by A Good Thing, Inc.
Cover design by Takeshi Takahashi
Cover printed by Art Print Company, Taylor, PA
Book printed and bound by Maple Press, York, PA
Date printed: November 2010

Printed in the United States of America

10 9 8 7 6 5 4 3 2 1

This book is printed on acid-free paper.

Contents

Foreword

To say that the motion picture industry has changed dramatically over the past 50 years is at best an understatement, and to say that there will be changes over the next 50 years—the likely course of your career—is not a prediction but a fact. It is clear that those of you near the beginning of your careers, for example, will work primarily in digital media and seldom, if at all, in 35 mm film. You may find yourselves working on features for Web casts and direct-to-home markets rather than theatrical distribution as the rising cost of real estate forces movie theaters to focus solely on productions with mass-market appeal. New technology has changed the motion picture industry before and it will continue to be a catalyst for change in the future. Now what would you say if I told you that this is not what matters?

It is obvious that you have to be aware of technological developments, which will influence your profession. At this stage in your career, however, I encourage you to look not outside at the industry but inside yourself. You cannot be wedded to a particular format because that format may change several times over the course of your career. You have to think about your talent, your skills, what you really want to do, and for what audience you want to do it. If you want to be a screenwriter, for example, there will always be some form of narrative filmmaking, whether the end product is distributed theatrically, on the Web, or in some as yet undefined format. Many of you probably think you know what you want to do: you have "always known" you want to direct, write, or produce. But during your first few jobs you need to see if you are really good enough to compete in that arena. You need to determine whether the day-to-day work in that profession is really what you want. The wonderful thing about the film industry is that there are so many different types of jobs, each of which can offer tremendous career satisfaction. You may discover that directing is not for you, but that you do have great ideas, a good sense of what the public likes, and excellent interpersonal skills. Maybe you would like to work for a studio as a development or creative executive. You may find that you really cannot deal with the often solitary life of a writer. But perhaps your early work experience will uncover leadership skills, facility with numbers, and good judgment. You might make a good producer.

The message here is that you should use your early work experiences as an opportunity for self-examination. Look at yourself critically. Learning what you are not good at is as important as discovering the areas in which you do excel. Most of the entry-level positions in filmmaking will put you either on the set as a production assistant or in the studio offices as a personal assistant. These jobs will allow you to see much of the filmmaking process and how the various roles interplay. That is why it is vital to work as much as you can and on as many different productions as you can. Do not consider any job too menial.

While self-assessment is essential during the formative years of your career, remember to always keep up with changes in your industry. You have chosen an industry famous for constant change, and you will have to be a constant learner in order to succeed. You will need to attend seminars, watch webcasts, join professional organizations, and read trade publications to keep up with changes that will influence the style, if not the substance, of your work. I also encourage you to spend an hour each week in relevant chat rooms on the Web. These can be the sites of brainstorming for the media's future. The technological developments that changed the film industry in the past were initiated by young entrepreneurs. You may be one of the new entrepreneurs who will change the industry yet again.

Woody Allen once said, "Eighty percent of success is showing up." I might add "and on time!" You have shown up here. Read this book. Ask questions of it and yourself. You will be surprised how many people there are out there who will help you answer the questions that you have.

—Peter Haratonik, Chair, Media Studies
NEW SCHOOL FOR SOCIAL RESEARCH
NEW YORK, NEW YORK

Acknowledgments

I would like to thank actor, screenwriter, and all-around film expert Bill Wilson for helping me get started and providing invaluable review and consultation throughout the process. The experts interviewed in this book—Mark Freeman, Howard Weinberg, and Frank Prinzi—all provided far more insight and advice than is reflected in the published interviews. I wish Peter Haratonik had been around when I began my career; his advice is useful even now. I am grateful to Ray Hubley who took time away from a tight deadline to share the "chemistry" of editing. I was lucky to have a terrific editor, Jeff Galas, who took time away from his vacation to guide me over some rough spots. Most of all, I want to thank my wonderful 13-year-old daughter, Anna, who abandoned typical teenage behavior and assumed many adult responsibilities whenever I was near a deadline.

Introduction

You probably already know that you do not bleed from shots and cuts, although the screen may bleed. You know that a wrap is not something used to cover a gift. Maybe you even know that cheating is not an ethical issue. But do you know not to call the police when someone yells, "Kill the baby!" Do you realize it is not sexual harassment when someone asks you to grab the redhead? Do you know not to run to the bar when the director shouts, "Martini!" The film industry is filled with two types of jargon—the language of the trade and the slang of the insiders. Knowing the former is essential to your credibility. Knowing the latter helps you sound like an experienced professional. *Career Launcher: Film* will tell you everything you need to know to sound like a pro your first day on the job. This book provides the background needed to fully understand the film industry, including how it developed, the challenges it faces today, who does what both on and off the set, and how to get ahead in your chosen career path.

The history of the motion picture industry is a fascinating history of the United States. The industry embraced immigrants and is built on invention and ingenuity. Chapter 1 traces this history from the days when motion pictures were one-minute peep shows to the blockbuster films of today. From the beginning there has been a conflict between the big studios with their blockbuster movies and the independent filmmakers struggling to tell their stories to a more limited audience. What becomes clear in this book, however, is that while the conflicts are often paramount in the media and in the minds of new filmmakers, these two sides of the industry have both flourished for many years. When one looks at the films produced over the past 60 years, a picture emerges of excellence in both Hollywood and the world of the independents.

Chapter 2 gives you an insider's look at the film industry today. You will see the structure of the studio system and you will learn how the different types of independent companies fit in. Independent filmmaking can range from one or two people struggling on their own to raise money to make a film to companies that regularly work with the major studios. This is the chapter that follows the money, revealing the wage and salary ranges of different types of work in addition to how much is spent and grossed by different types of productions. Another important aspect of this chapter is the discussion of how the economics of the motion picture industry has impacted the national economy by providing jobs for local residents and using the services of small businesses across the country. Although the industry is concentrated in Hollywood and, to a lesser extent, New York, Chapter 2 shows that there are jobs available in almost every state.

Chapter 3 organizes the jobs according to the filmmaking process—development, preproduction, production, and postproduction—and the administrative jobs, including management and support. Many positions cross over and are involved with multiple phases of filmmaking and with the executive side as well. Chapter 3 shows how people in different positions work with each other and some of the paths people may follow. This chapter may expose you to different things you would like to try, and it will help you to understand the work of everyone around you.

Chapter 4 addresses the most pressing concerns of anyone in any business, but especially in film. How do you get ahead? It dispels the myth that you must know someone influential in the business to get a foot in the door or to progress to a higher level. But it shows that getting to know people during your early years is the single most important factor in determining your future. In an industry where people are primarily hired project-by-project, making connections and doing a good job will lead you from one film to the next for a particular director or producer. Chapter 4 shows you the right way to network, how to handle yourself on the set, and how to pursue industry contacts met at seminars or events. It offers specific time-tested advice to help you find a mentor to guide your career.

Chapter 4 will also help you plan your career. Many of the successful filmmakers interviewed for this book urge people to move around early in their careers, to do anything to get a foot in the door, to experiment with as many different types of work as possible. But it is not a good idea to do that for too long. Frank Prinzi, ASC, a successful cinematographer featured in Chapter 4, cautions that once you know the business, you need to set a goal and start to work toward it. Once you have been in the film business a few years it is time to think about what you have learned about yourself, about your likes and dislikes, and about your strengths and weaknesses. It is then time to plan subsequent jobs that will specifically train you for the position you ultimately want.

The extensive glossary in Chapter 5 is written for people in all positions, from entry level to professional, from the set to the executive suite. Industry veterans sometimes entertain themselves on the set by using jargon that is unfamiliar to most entry level people. If this happens to you, know that it is part of the process—an initiation of sorts—and try to laugh at yourself. Then study Chapter 5 so that it does not happen again.

Resources that can help you further your career are outlined in Chapter 6. In addition to the many books and Web sites discussed, there is a list of unions and guilds, which play a big role in every aspect of the business—there is the Screen Actors Guild, Writers Guild of America, Directors Guild of America, Producers Guild of America, and International Alliance of Theatrical and Stage Employees, to name a few. In a field where employment is primarily on a project-by-project basis, the unions play an especially important role, and they are often a great source of information. In addition to the bargaining power traditionally associated with unions, these unions usually offer health insurance and other benefits normally provided by a full time employer. Chapter 6 is also filled with lists to help you find out about film festivals, events, and job openings.

In all, we hope this book will give you the extra help you need in the early years of your career to feel as comfortable as a pro, to identify your long-term career goals, and to plot out a path to those goals.

Chapter 1

Industry History

Filmmaking gives us a picture of our society. It helps us understand our past, cope with our present, and it gives us a window to our future. Filmmaking may also be the art form with the greatest potential to change society, to hold up a mirror to social wrongs and give us the impetus for meaningful change. The motion picture industry that we extol (and critique) today is as distinctly an American phenomenon as hot dogs and baseball. The early technological developments that made the industry possible were as much French as American, and several other countries soon joined in with technological and artistic advances. But the history of filmmaking as it has unfolded in the United States could only happen in America.

In the early days of the industry, developments in film technologies in the United States and France paralleled each other. Then the paths diverged. Why? The film industry in the United States was predicated on the profit motive, and the government-supported film industry in Europe was predicated on art. Lack of government support for the arts may not have had a significant impact on the development of literature, fine arts, or music, but it has dramatically impacted film because filmmaking is based on technology, and technology is expensive. The need for technology and funding set the film industry apart from other forms of art. Although these forces have limited creative expression on occasion, they have also created a medium available to everyone, not just a socioeconomic elite. The need for collaboration also differentiates the film industry from other forms of art, producing what one might call "group art," which reflects the vision of a writer, director, and actors. Success in the film industry means the artist must leave the ivory tower to maneuver in the world of business and finance.

From a Galloping Horse to an Oncoming Train: The Early Days of Motion Pictures, 1878–1915

The late 19th century and early 20th century was a period of rapid growth in technology, art, and business. The film industry began in 1878 in Palo Alto, California, as Sallie Gardner, a horse, galloped past 24 stereoscopic cameras. Eadweard Muybridge photographed Sallie in rapid motion as her hooves triggered each camera shutter, taking pictures one thousandth of a second apart.

The race to develop the technology for motion pictures was on. The chief contender in the United States was Thomas Edison, along with his chief engineer William Kennedy Laurie Dickson. Dickson invented a useable form of a celluloid strip. Edison then designed the Kinetograph, the first actual moving-picture camera, and the Kinetoscope, a cabinet in which a continuous loop of Dickson's celluloid film, powered by an electric motor, was backlit by an incandescent lamp and projected through a magnifying lens. Viewers watched short films through an eyepiece. Kinetoscope parlors, or peep show parlors, spread rapidly throughout the United States and Europe. Films focused on everyday events—imagine going to see a film called *Fred Ott's Sneeze*—and vaudeville style entertainment.

The idea of projecting images for group viewing originated with Robert W. Paul in Great Britain and the Lumiére brothers in France. Auguste and Louis Lumiére invented the Cinematographé, a camera, printer, and projector all in one. On December 28, 1895, the Lumiére brothers used their Cinematographé to project short films to a paying audience of 35 in the Grand Café in Paris. One of the films showed a train coming into the station. Mark Freeman, an award-winning documentary filmmaker and professor at the School of Theater, Television, and Film at San Diego State University, says it has been reported (though not confirmed) that viewers ran from the café as the train entered the station. Freeman explains that the Lumiére brothers wanted to "bring the world to the world." They and most other filmmakers of the time focused on "actualities," films portraying lives of others in exotic locations—North Africa, Asia, and czarist Russia, for example. Edison and the Lumiére brothers are generally credited as the inventors of motion pictures, according to Freeman, but he notes that scientists and engineers in Great Britain, Germany, France, and the United States independently designed components and various manifestations of the camera and projector.

Films were first shown at vaudeville shows and other events, but in 1905 the Nickelodeon, the first movie theater, opened in Pittsburgh, and within a few years thousands of nickelodeons had sprung up around the country. Films at this time were nothing like what we have come to know as movies today. Only a few minutes long at most, these films had no camera movement, no editing, and no synchronized sound or dialogue.

The ability to make money by offering inexpensive mass entertainment was almost instantly apparent, and motion picture companies sprung up while scientists and engineers sought ways to improve production values. As new technology came on the scene so did patent wars over the mechanisms that made movies possible. Then, after years of feuding over patents, in 1908 the major American filmmaking companies—Edison, Biograph, Pathe, Vitagraph, Lubin, Selig, Esssanay, Kalem, and the Kleine Optical Company—pooled their patents and formed the Motion Picture Patents Company (MPPC), a trust aimed at controlling the American film business. Better known as the Edison Trust, the MPPC charged fees to all distributors and exhibitors, and Eastman Kodak agreed to supply film stock only to MPPC members. It was this attempt at a monopoly that drove the seat of the film business from New York to California. In early 1913 it was difficult to extend legal reach across the country, so independent filmmakers fled to Southern California. Once there they realized the filming advantages of year-round good weather and wide-open spaces, and California became the permanent seat of the industry.

Meanwhile, filmmakers experimented with ways to make films more interesting and more marketable. Filmmaking progressed from a single static shot to the beginnings of many of the techniques used today. Scenes were filmed from a moving train and a rotating camera head was designed to create the first rudimentary panning shots. Cutaway shots were used and simple editing began. A stop-motion technique was used to make a woman vanish, and double exposure of film created a ghost effect. The first films made using reverse motion were *Tipsy, Topsy, Turvy* and *The Awkward Sign Painter*. What we now call single frame animation or pixilation was first used to

On the Cutting
Edge

How the Studios Dealt with New Technology

In *This Business of Film: A Practical Guide to Achieving Success in the Film Industry*, authors Stephen Greenwald and Paula Landry observe a four-stage pattern in the way Hollywood has responded to new technology: (1) fear; (2) attempt to crush; (3) test the waters, involving external companies to minimize financial risk; (4) make it a profit center.

Television: When television came on the scene in the early 1950s, the studio heads thought it was all over for them. Then Lew Wasserman, chair of MCA Universals, had an idea. Why not recycle old movies? Take them out of the warehouse, dust them off, and get them to make money again. He began selling rights to these movies to television. Then the studios set up production arms geared specifically to television.

Cable TV: As cable TV gained popularity, the film industry tried to take it over by starting its own channel, Premiere, and giving it exclusive pay-TV licensing rights to films from the main studios—Paramount, Universal, Columbia, and Fox. The courts intervened to

create moving intertitles in 1905. Intertitles, or title cards, contained printed text for dialogue or narration and were used to help viewers follow the story as silent films grew in length and complexity. These title cards were inserted in the middle of the screen in contrast to subtitles, which run along the bottom.

The basic technique for the cartoon animation used today dates to a 1906 film in which Albert Edward Smith and James Stuart Blackton made cartoon characters appear to move by altering the drawings. There were attempts to create continuity of action, and reverse angle cutting was done for the first time. The use of artificial light was expanded and silhouette effects were used. Filmmakers made rudimentary attempts at cross-cutting between parallel actions, point-of-view shots, and reverse-angle cutting. As filmmakers sought to tell prevent the film industry's attempt at monopoly. The film industry began to license films for pay TV and this soon became a significant source of revenue.

VCRs: Film executives feared that VCRs would cause them to lose income from the licensing of theatrical films for broadcast and cable television. They attempted to enjoin the sale of VCRs on the grounds that they could be used to illegally copy films. When manufacturers won this suit, the studios initially held back from offering video rights to their films. Eventually the studios began to test the water by offering licensing rights to intermediary video distributors. Then as the home video market grew, the studios cut out the intermediaries and established their own in-house divisions to license video rights directly to wholesalers and retailers. Within a few years the intermediary distributors were out of business and the film industry's biggest profit center was from home video licensing and sales.

DVDs: As DVD sales quickly went through the roof, so did the studios' licensing of films. In 2006, home viewing was the largest source of income for the film industry and the source for almost half its profits.

stories, they began to use flashbacks, symbolism, insert shots, and intertitles to help the audience follow the story in their silent films. Although many of the early films were not focused around a story-line, the trend toward storytelling began early and has continued. The beginnings of narrative construction expanded opportunities for writers, whether they were scripting shows or adapting novels.

As the American story played out, filmmaking grew around the world as well. In 1908 in France, a new company, Film d'Art, began making films using artists renowned for their work in theater, and adapting stories from classic literature. The term "art film" was coined. British and German production expanded. The industry grew in Italy with a focus on the historic epic and on slapstick as well. The film industry grew in Denmark, later in Sweden, and in

Russia. In 1910, however, American films maintained the largest market share in European countries as well as in the United States because of their technical superiority

The *Birth of a Nation*, the Start of a War: 1915–1927

A pivotal year for filmmaking, 1915 marks the first dramatic advance in the use of film to tell a complex story. D. W. Griffith's *Birth of a Nation* is a Civil War story told from the point of view of a racist white southerner. Controversy about this film has continued for almost 100 years, from the National Association for the Advancement of Colored People's (NAACP) protests at its release to the current dilemmas faced by film school professors over showing the film in class. In his book, *God, Man and Hollywood: Politically Incorrect Cinema from* The Birth of a Nation *to* The Passion of the Christ, Mark Winchell contends that—as the first film to tell a coherent story and to masterfully use cinematic and editing techniques to convey emotion—*Birth of a Nation* is the most influential film of all time. Yet, says Winchell, it is rarely shown to film students because of the inflammatory treatment of race relations. However, *Birth of a Nation* was a box office hit and set the stage for full-length feature films that tell a novel-like story.

Perhaps because they did not yet have sound to focus on, great directors of the silent period made sweeping advances in cinematography. They developed techniques to demonstrate character emotion without sound. These included better and more use of point-of-view shots (POV) and symbolism. Insert shots, such as close-ups of wringing hands, tapping feet, or a revolver became commonplace. Cecil B. DeMille, one of the leading directors of this period, used about nine insert shots in every 100 shots in *The Whispering Chorus*. DeMille also used these shots to infuse sensuality into his films. For example, in the 1918 film *Old Wives for New*, DeMille showed a close-up of a silver-plated gun amidst a bunch of silky, sexy ribbons. In *Whispering*, DeMille also effectively used cross-cutting to show a supposedly dead husband liaising with a prostitute while his "widow" is being remarried in Church. Around this time Griffith used cross-cutting to tell four parallel stories in the film *Intolerance*. This structure turned out to be too complex, and *Intolerance* was a box office flop. Hence subsequent films had simpler structures. An early example of an atmospheric insert came from Maurie Tourneur in *The Pride of the*

Clan, which used waves coming in on a rocky shore to depict the story's location. This was a period of great directors perfecting the cinematography of storytelling. In addition to Griffith, DeMille, and Tourneur, some directors of the period included Erich von Stroheim, Sidney Drew, Fatty Arbuckle, and the inimitable Charles Chaplin. Ernst Lubitsch of Germany, America's prime filmmaking competitor of the time, and the Spanish surrealist Luis Buñuel made major advances in cinematography.

American films were at the forefront of the industry in this period as earlier, this time because European countries were more impacted by World War I. In addition, federal courts dissolved the MPPC, ruling that it was an illegal monopoly, allowing more people in to the industry. Although filmmakers were no longer inhibited by the strength of a monopoly, they still had to compete with the rapidly developing studio system. As major studios emerged, they began to control not only production but distribution and exhibition as well. The age of the celebrity began. Studio heads who had previously treated actors like disposable props suddenly realized that certain people were big box office draws. Although this led to greater compensation and special treatment for leading actors, they were still employees of the studio and they had very restrictive contracts.

At this time the "Big Five" studios—Warner Bros., Paramount, RKO, Metro-Goldwyn-Mayer, and the Fox Film Corporation/Foundation—owned everything: production companies, distribution companies, theaters, and all talent (actors, writers, directors, and producers). This business model would last until the 1950s.

The Golden Age of Hollywood: From the First Talkies to TV

Expensive, new technology secured the dominance of the Big Five. Although people had been tinkering with synchronized sound for quite some time, the silent era ended abruptly and completely with *The Jazz Singer* in 1927. From that point on, people only wanted to see films with dialogue, and producers who could not afford the new technology went out of business. But even the Big Five could not afford this expensive new technology on their own. As they began to bring in investors, the need for profitability usurped artistic expression and quieted individual voices. Keeping investors happy was paramount. Movies had to be box office hits. That meant they had to appeal to the widest possible audience. They also had to appeal to the socially conservative views of investors. The theme of small-town, hard-working America was in; sexuality was out. "Prior to this, movies were often racy with mature themes," says Freeman. The studios began to move toward self-censorship by forming The Motion Picture Producers and Distributors of America in 1922. Better known as the Hays Office, after its head, William H. Hays, this entity made sure married couples slept in separate beds, breasts were covered, and bad language was never spoken.

Studio heads reigned supreme. In *God, Man and Hollywood* Winchell describes the Hollywood of the 1930s through the 1950s as "a fiefdom run by vulgar, avaricious, semiliterate studio heads." With the exception of the superstars, actors, writers, and directors were treated "like serfs," according to Winchell. Writers generally fared worse than actors since they were not visible and studio heads saw them as interchangeable. No wonder many of the writers of this period saw themselves as the "exploited proletariat" and joined the Communist Party, laying the groundwork for events that would shake Hollywood to its core in the 1950s.

You might say that the Allies and the Axis powers were fighting World War II with films as well as with guns. The Office of War Information supported several propaganda films with excellent cinematic values, directors, and cast. Frank Capra's *Why We Fight* (1943) was not a patriotic flag-waving film, but rather a serious attempt to show the devastation of war and the difficulties in overcoming the Axis powers. Other propaganda films included *Desperate Journey* (1942)—featuring leading man Errol Flynn as the hero pitted against Raymond Massey and Ronald Reagan as Nazis—*Mrs. Miniver, Forever and a Day,* and *Objective Burma.* On the other side was Leni Riefenstahl with her German propaganda film *Triumph des Willens* (Triumph of the Will, 1934). Similar to the controversy over D.W. Griffith's racist theme in a groundbreaking film, the content of Riefenstahl's work was reprehensible as were her known friendships with Adolph Hitler and Joseph Goebbels. The quality of her cinematography, on the other hand, was way ahead of its time. Riefenstahl was first to use cranes and many cameras working simultaneously. During World War II, filmmakers sought to reflect society and to influence the course of events.

At this time, the Soviet Union was an ally. Many investors were unable to see anything but the positive in the Soviet Union, and they ignored signs that this relationship might change some day. Studios turned out films extolling the virtues of the country. *Song of Russia* (1944) and *North Star* (1948) portrayed an idyllic image of Soviet life. *Mission to Moscow* glorified Stalin's acts of oppression and the show trials of the late 1930s.

But in spite of greedy studio heads, self-serving investors, ill-treated creative talent, and a world war, Hollywood turned out some great films in the 1930s and 1940s. As technology advanced, different film genres emerged—musicals, gangster films, and Disney's animated adventures. The first Hollywood musical was *The Broadway Melody*, 1929, while *42nd Street* premiered in 1933.

King Kong, Dracula, and Frankenstein were all born in the 1930s. It was a period of contrasts, with something for everyone. There were gangster films, like *The Public Enemy*; comedy, such as *The Front Page*; the slapstick of the Marx Brothers; and the animated classics of Walt Disney. Two all-time classics appeared in 1939, *The Wizard of Oz* and David O. Selznick's *Gone with the Wind*. Interestingly, *Gone with the Wind* could have spurred the protests which compromised *Birth of a Nation* had it not been for Selznick's removal of the Ku Klux Klan from the script. Other derogatory terms were debated and some left in. Racism was present not only in the film but in the filmmaking. Clark Gable threatened to walk off the set because of the segregated bathrooms. The bathrooms were desegregated and Rhett Butler got to say, "Frankly Scarlett, I don't give a damn."

In the 1940s, World War II gave birth to realistic drama, such as *Watch on the Rhine* and *Shadow of a Doubt*, and to escape through fantasy—*Yankee Doodle Dandy* and *It's a Wonderful Life* (which still runs on television at least once each year around Christmas). This was the decade of Orson Welles's *Citizen Kane*, still considered one of the greatest films ever made; *Casablanca*, as loved today as it was over 70 years ago; and *The Maltese Falcon*. While most talent was ill treated, superstars enjoyed unsurpassed luxury—Humphrey Bogart, Clark Gable, and Katharine Hepburn, to name a few. This was also the time of Shirley Temple.

American cinema was center stage because of the costs involved and the impact of the war on other countries. Nevertheless, some noteworthy films came out of Great Britain and Europe. Great Britain turned out realistic war dramas like the *49th Parallel*; comedies, such as *The Man in the White Suit*; and trend-setting thrillers, like *The Third Man*. Italian neorealism began in 1943 with *Obsessions*.

In the 1930s and 1940s, Hollywood was big, it was powerful, and it was ruled by money—but it created films that changed the direction of filmmaking and that still influence us today. This was the Golden Age of Hollywood. It was a time to remember, particularly during the trials and tribulations of the coming decade.

Fighting Television and Congress: The 1950s

Two major threats hit the motion picture industry in the late 1940s and the 1950s: The House Un-American Activities Committee and television. The Soviet Union moved from ally to enemy and two acts of treason—Alger Hiss and the Rosenbergs—rocked the nation. The "exploited proletariat" of writers and directors who had joined the Communist Party to support their egalitarian ideals and to defend themselves against crude, avaricious studio heads were now seen as a threat to national security. The House committee was looking for communists under every rock, and they searched hard through Hollywood. Actors, directors, and writers who were called to testify before this committee had to prove their loyalty to the country by naming others who might be communists or face being blacklisted, held in contempt of Congress, and/or jailed. Tight-lipped heroes emerged and many of them were jailed and blacklisted. Unable to work in the United States, some fled to the United Kingdom and Europe. The Hollywood Ten, those brave artists who went to jail rather than name names, were Alvah Bessie, Herbert J. Biberman, Lester Cole, Edward Dmytryk, Ring Lardner, Jr., John Howard Lawson, Albert Maltz, Samuel Ornitz, Adrian Scott, and Dalton Trumbo. After spending time in jail, these men were blacklisted and could not work in Hollywood for quite some time. Some wrote using pseudonyms until the political climate changed. The paranoia of this era is reflected in films such as *Invasion of the Body Snatchers, The War of the Worlds,* and *The Manchurian Candidate.*

While fighting the congressional witch hunt, the motion picture industry faced a technological challenge as well, one they believed would ruin them. Studio executives feared that people would not want to go out to the movies once they had the option of watching television at home. Theater attendance declined and some theaters went bankrupt and closed.

Hollywood tried to compete with TV by creating Cinemascope screens and producing movie spectaculars meant for the big screen. Epic films included *The Robe* (1953), *War and Peace* (1955), *The Ten*

Fast Facts

The Top 10 Box Office Hits of All Time

	U.S. Box Office
1. *Avatar*	$749,073,100
2. *Titanic* (1997)	$600,779,824
3. *The Dark Knight* (2008)	$533,316,061
4. *Star Wars* (1977)	$460,935,665
5. *Shrek 2* (2004)	$436,471,036
6. *ET: The Extra-Terrestrial* (1982)	$434,949,459
7. *Star Wars Episode I: The Phantom Menace* (1999)	$431,065,444
8. *Pirates of the Caribbean: Dead Man's Chest* (2006)	$432,032,628
9. *Spider-Man* (2002)	$403,706,375
10. *Star Wars Episode III: Revenge of the Sith* (2005)	$380,262,555

Source: http://www.imdb.com/boxoffice/alltimegross

Commandments (1956), *Around the World in 80 Days* (1956), *Ben Hur* (1959), and *Lawrence of Arabia* (1962). Major animated Disney classics came out during this period: *Cinderella, Peter Pan, Lady and the Tramp,* and *Sleeping Beauty.* The industry also tried to lure audience with gimmicks, such as 3D, which failed. But there were also hits that have stood the test of time, such as *Singin' in the Rain* (1952).

Then the motion picture industry figured out how to make what they feared work to their advantage, and by the late 1950s the studios were profiting nicely from licensing old films and producing new ones for television. In *This Business of Film*, Stephen Greenwald and Paula Landry observe that this was a scenario that would play out repeatedly in the future, each time new technology was introduced. The studios would first perceive the new technology as a threat and try to squash it. Then gingerly they would approach it, trying to get their feet wet without drowning—in other words, getting others to take the financial risks. Finally, the studios would take over and enjoy another new profit center.

In spite of having to deal with threats of a blacklist and jail, in spite of having to figure out how to survive in the wake of television, filmmakers did what they do best. They produced important films that reflected the issues with which society was beginning to grapple, most notably the beginning of the civil rights movement. Films addressing race relations and other social issues included *Blackboard Jungle, On the Waterfront, Marty,* and *Twelve Angry Men.* In 1962, viewers flocked to see *To Kill a Mockingbird,* the story of Atticus Finch, a principled white attorney who defends a black man falsely accused of raping a white woman. The coming demise of the studio system could be predicted with films like *Sunset Boulevard* and *The Bad and the Beautiful.* The latter focused on the sordid and sad aspects of the system, with Kirk Douglas playing the egotistical producer who controlled and cheated those around him. In *Sunset Boulevard,* William Holden and Gloria Swanson revealed the struggles of a writer and an actress trying to find their way back in the system.

The late 1950s and early 1960s was also the time of one of the greatest directors of all time—Alfred Hitchcock. After a successful career in the United Kingdom during the silent era and with early talkies, Hitchcock migrated to Hollywood. There he raised the bar for suspense with films like *Rear Window* (1954), *Vertigo* (1958), *North by Northwest* (1959), *Psycho* (1960), and *The Birds* (1963). Hitchcock produced *Psycho,* one of the most revered films of all time, with a budget of $800,000. With a sparse set he created tension that sent screams through the audience. But Hitchcock's films were not just thrillers; they were commentaries on society, on human relationships, on the human condition.

This was also a significant period for filmmaking in India and Japan. India turned out over 200 films in the 1950s, including some that would have a major impact on future filmmaking, such as *Pather Panchali* or *Song of the Little Road.* Japanese cinema produced films still famous today, such as *Rashomon* and *The Seven Samurai.*

Finally, the changes occurring in this decade set the stage for the demise of the studio system as it existed in the 1940s and for the birth of opportunities for independent filmmakers. The major studios were prohibited from supplying films to their own distributors after a 1948 Supreme Court decision in *United States v. Paramount Pictures,* a government antitrust action against the major studios. This decision, combined with the trend to produce fewer, but bigger, films because of television, made it too expensive to keep all creative talent on staff.

The studio heads let go of their restrictive contracts with directors, actors, and writers because they were no longer producing enough movies to keep them in salaried positions. As the studios moved from employing talent to hiring them on a contract basis, these actors, directors, and writers were free to start their own companies or work for television. Although this seemed to have the potential to weaken the studios, it actually made them stronger. The new independent companies brought their projects to the studios for financing and distribution (making the new companies a bit less "independent"). Similarly, the television they feared became their friend as well. In the coming decades as theater sales declined, profits from television increased to take their place. By the 1960s the model of an all-powerful studio system controlling every aspect of filmmaking, from production through distribution, was on its way out. Hollywood studios were morphing in to a new model, one in which independent filmmakers and television would replace income lost from declining theater sales.

The Era When Everything Changed: The 1960s–1980s

Society was in turmoil. Martin Luther King, Jr., and the civil rights movement awakened America's conscience. A new president challenged young people to "Ask not what your country can do for you, ask what you can do for your country." Neither leader made it through the 1960s: John F. Kennedy was assassinated in 1963, and King in 1968. A new generation protested the war in Vietnam and began challenging society's attitudes toward sex, race, and gender. It was an era of change, of challenge, of contrasts in society and in the movies. It was an era where Hollywood held its own, independents began to flourish, and foreign films drew large U.S. audiences.

In the 1960s, Hollywood was there for those who wanted comfort and escape from the rapidly changing landscape. Hollywood clung to the past with family movies, such as *Mary Poppins*, *My Fair Lady*, and *The Sound of Music*. There were exceptions, however. In *The Hustler* (1961), Paul Newman created a flawed character, struggling with his own psyche and his desire for change. John Cassavetes, a former Hollywood actor, became the "father of independent cinema" with films that spoke out against social convention and self-deception. Cassavetes focused more on character than on plot. To avoid their influence, he took no financing from banks or major studios.

INTERVIEW

Filmmaking: Yesterday and Today

Mark Freeman
Professor in the School of Theater, Television, and Film at San Diego State University, San Diego, California; award-winning documentary filmmaker

When did you become a documentary filmmaker and which hats do you personally wear in the filmmaking process?
I began making films about 30 years ago. In many of my productions, I wear all the hats. I formulate the idea, research the material, write, produce, direct, shoot, and edit. I also raise funds.

How would you characterize your productions?
I tell stories about ordinary people trying to make a difference in their world. *Talking Peace*, for example, portrays Jews and Palestinians in San Diego striving for open dialogue and hoping to influence peace-making efforts. *Edmund's Island* is the story of a homeless news hawker who is an angel to his customers.

Why have you chosen a career as a documentary filmmaker and educator?
I believe filmmaking has tremendous power and can make a difference in our lives and in our world. I believe motion pictures influence the way we think and act.

What do you see as the underlying purpose of filmmaking?
Filmmaking, whether nonfiction or fiction, is about storytelling. From the days of cave painting, we have used images to tell stories about

However, he had trouble funding his productions, such as *Faces* and *Shadows*, and had to rely on overseas distribution. Cassavetes was first to use an interracial couple on the big screen. Meanwhile across the Atlantic, filmmakers were also breaking the rules and generating an increasing audience in the United States. Innovative and popular directors of this period included Francois Truffaut and Jean-Luc Godard of the French New Wave, Federico Fellini from Italy, and Ingmar Bergman from Sweden. Great Britain's films reflected the trend toward more open sexuality and broke the bans ourselves, about what it is to be human. From the early "actualities" to the present time, filmmaking has given us a way to look at ourselves and our society.

Why is *Birth of a Nation* considered so important to the history of filmmaking?

D. W. Griffith introduced complex storytelling over an expanse of time and space. In 1915, Griffith's use of parallel editing distinguished *Birth of a Nation* as groundbreaking. He used cutting to heighten emotion, not just to condense time and space.

What role did the silent film era play in the society of the early 1900s?

The lack of synchronized sound technology may have made films more useful to society at that time. Thirteen million immigrants flooded into U.S. urban areas between 1900 and 1914. The short, "silent" films were inexpensive and accessible to these new Americans. They were understandable to people who did not yet know the language. Silent films helped orient newcomers to American culture while providing entertainment.

How do you envision the future for independent filmmakers?

Independent filmmakers have always searched for new opportunities to reach diverse audiences. Cable promised public access and 500 channels, VCRs and DVDs made duplication cheap and easy, the digital revolution dramatically lowered the costs of production and postproduction, and the Internet offered unlimited global distribution. But in some ways the more things change, the more they have stayed the same. As thousands of filmmakers compete to become the next viral phenomenon, many worthy films and filmmakers still remain overlooked and underappreciated.

on nudity. *Alfie*, *Blowup*, and *Georgy Girl* drew huge U.S. audiences. The United Kingdom also produced several realistic dramas from the "Free Cinema" and the highly unrealistic first James Bond movie, *Dr. No* (1962). Films from Africa, politically focused films from Latin America, and films from Japan, most notably Kurosawa's *Yojimbo*, were also popular in the United States. By the end of the decade even Hollywood started turning out films that reflected the social unrest of the time—*Bonnie and Clyde*, *Rosemary's Baby*, *The Graduate*, *Midnight Cowboy*, *Easy Rider*, and *2001: A Space Odyssey*.

As the studio system declined, so did the self-censorship overseen by the Hays Office. In 1966, Jack Valenti, president of the Motion Picture Association of America, replaced the old production code with a ratings system. The new code, which took effect in 1968, consisted of four categories and was a forerunner for the code used today.

By the 1970s, the United States joined Europe and began experimenting with sexual content, nudity, and graphic violence. The notion of clearly defined "good" and "evil" characters in films gave way to shades of gray as anti-heroes, such as the likeable Butch Cassidy and the Sundance Kid, became less perfect and protagonists were not all evil. Controversial films of the early 1970s included *Straw Dogs*, *A Clockwork Orange*, *The French Connection*, and *Dirty Harry*. In 1970, *Patton* focused more on the complexities of the general's character than on his feats in war.

No longer employed and controlled by studios, "auteur" directors came of age. Martin Scorsese, Francis Ford Coppola, Steven Spielberg, George Lucas, and Brian DePalma began experimenting and produced notable films, such as Scorsese's *Taxi Driver*, Coppola's *Godfather* trilogy, Spielberg's *Jaws*, and Lucas's *Star Wars*. The box office success of films like *Jaws* and *Star Wars* heralded the trend toward fewer but higher-budget films with extraordinary special effects. The 1970s also gave birth to more pornographic films, which ultimately moved to home media with video and cable. West German films gained popularity in the United States, as did martial arts films. Although the era of the Hollywood musical was over, the Bollywood musical era was just beginning. Musicals from India became popular in the United States, and this genre is still popular in India today.

Meanwhile, another auteur director was getting his start with perhaps the most famous romantic comedy of all time, *Annie Hall*. Woody Allen began experimenting with different styles and different genres, and his films usually generated an acceptable audience on the coasts. There are stories that video shops put his movies in the foreign films section, and he was in fact largely influenced by Fellini and Bergman. Whether the movie was mostly comedy or drama, Allen looked at existential questions and focused on what it means to be human.

Interestingly, the biggest blows to the growth of independent filmmaking in the 1970s came from a director who would go on to produce independent, thought-provoking films in the 1990s. But in 1975, Steven Spielberg produced one of the major blockbusters of all time, *Jaws*. Two years later, George Lucas broke box office records with *Star Wars*. The age of the blockbuster, saturation marketing, and merchandising began.

Contrasts became even more pronounced in the 1980s. Hollywood played it safe with sequels to its blockbuster hits, while independents started generating much larger audiences. There were two more *Star Wars*, three more *Jaws*, several more *Rocky's*, and three *Indiana Jones* films, all box office successes. In addition, Michael J. Fox went *Back to the Future* three times. In 1989, *Batman* broke all box-office records. Disney's *Tron*, the first large screen film to use computer graphics exclusively, was released in 1982. But the studios also released major unconventional films, such as *Raging Bull*, *The King of Comedy*, and *Scarface*. Independent filmmakers who began reaching large, popular audiences included the Coen brothers, David Lynch, and John Sayles. It was at this time that Robert Redford created the Sundance Institute.

The auteur director who best illustrated the period of change and turmoil from the 1960s through the 1980s was undoubtedly Oliver Stone. Awarded a Bronze Star for gallantry and a Purple Heart for his actions in Vietnam, Stone returned to the United States and showed the rest of the country that war was not a musical comedy. Stone did not put any gauze over the lens, revealing the pain and suffering of the Vietnam war in *Platoon* (1986) and *Born on the Fourth of July* (1989). With *Wall Street* (1987) he urged society to look at greed and corruption 20 years before it caused the collapse of the financial and auto industries in the United States.

At the same time, British cinema was attracting large U.S. audiences: *Chariots of Fire*, *Gandhi*, *The Killing Fields*, and *A Room with a View* appealed to those whose interests were not reflected in many of the Hollywood releases. Taking different approaches, Japanese and Hong Kong cinema both experienced revivals in the 1980s. Japanese anime films became popular, topped by *Akira* (1988) by Katsuhiro Otomo. Hong Kong's revitalization was led by a new type of action film exemplified by Jackie Chan, who combined comedic martial arts with heart-stopping stunts.

A Motion Picture Melting Pot: The 1990s to the Present

Although Hollywood still is and may always be the film capital of the world, it is no longer the center of all the action. Changes that began in the 1990s have decentralized the film industry in a variety

Everyone

Knows

Directors Who Changed the Art of Filmmaking

These are the names you will hear bantered about on the set and off. Everyone talks about these directors, and many of the techniques used in filmmaking today can be traced back to one of them. To develop this list, *MovieMakers* polled a panel of directors, writers, actors, critics, and others.

1. Alfred Hitchcock (1899–1980)
2. D.W. Griffith (1875–1948)
3. Orson Welles (1915–1985)
4. Jean-Luc Godard (1930–)
5. John Ford (1894–1973)
6. Stanley Kubrick (1928–1999)
7. Sergei Eisenstein (1898–1948)
8. Charlie Chaplin (1889–1997)
9. Federico Fellini (1920–1993)
10. Steven Spielberg (1946–)
11. Martin Scorsese (1942–)

of ways. First, several mergers and acquisitions have unseated the all-powerful studios and turned them into mere divisions of mega-conglomerates, which include movies, TV, music, publishing, live theater, theme parks, and other interests. Film divisions ended up pretty low on the totem pole in terms of revenues for these conglom-erates, so their managers hesitated to take risks that might negatively impact the parent company's stock price. To reduce risk, the execu-tives focused on proven box office draws—popular stars, remakes, sequels, and film versions of TV shows. Second, production decen-tralized as location shooting became more popular than the use of studio sets. Third, rather than producing all of their own movies, the studios often served as financiers for independent film companies.

12. Akira Kurosawa (1910–1998)

13. Ingmar Bergman (1918–)

14. John Cassavetes (1929–1989)

15. Billy Wilder (1906–2002)

16. Jean Renoir (1894–1979)

17. Francis Ford Coppola (1939–)

18. Howard Hawks (1896–1977)

19. Francois Truffaut (1932–1984)

20. Buster Keaton (1895–1996)

21. Fritz Lang (1890–1976)

22. John Huston (1906–1987)

23. Woody Allen (1935–)

24. Luis Bunuel (1900–1983)

25. Ernst Lubitsch (1892–1947)

Source: "Movie Makers Blue Chip Panel Names the 25 Most Influential Directors of All Time," by Jennifer Wood, July 6, 2002. http://www.moviemaker.com/directing/article/the_25_most_influential_directors_of_all_time

In addition to all of this, the industry decentralized by becoming more global. Although U.S. films had always had a substantial audience overseas, and foreign films had been gaining in popularity in the United States for quite some time, American film companies now began financing films by foreign directors like Ang Lee (*Crouching Tiger, Hidden Dragon*). Joint ventures between U.S. and foreign companies increased as well, such as Fox's partnership with Bollywood's UTV children's channel and Time Warner's venture with China Film Group.

As the industry decentralized the types of films made became more diverse. The past two decades have ushered in the most expensive film extravaganzas ever made in Hollywood and the cheapest, most innovative, and thought-provoking dramas. In the 1990s, the introduction of computer-designed digital special effects became the most significant technological advance since sound. Just as sound cemented the narrative construction of films, special effects introduced epic extravaganzas where the power was as much in the visual effect as in the story. Critics and viewers alike commented as much on the effect as on the story, the plot, and the characters. Most cinematic techniques serve as the punctuation marks for film. Viewers or readers do not really notice the close-ups and dissolves, for example. They just make the story clearer, the emotion more vivid. But special effects are not punctuation. They are the thing in and of themselves. Story line, message, and philosophical meaning took second seat to effects in epic films like *Pirates of the Caribbean: Dead Man's Chest, Terminator 2*, and *Indiana Jones and the Kingdom of the Crystal Skull*. These epics cost a fortune to produce and had to make a fortune to succeed. They did.

On the other side of town, inexpensive productions were appealing to larger audiences. In 1989, Steven Soderbergh made *Sex, Lies and Videotape*, a character-driven film, for $1 million. It reaped $24 million at the box office. Miramax Films—a successful independent company bought by Disney in 1993—released the provocative, controversial hit film *Pulp Fiction* in 1994. Then, in 1999 Daniel Myrick and Eduardo Sanchez directed and wrote *The Blair Witch Project*, a very low budget horror film that became a box office hit. Initial production costs were just $30,000. (Later it cost $100,000 for finishing and $320,000 for sound and color correction.) Shown at the 1999 Sundance Film Festival, it was immediately picked up by Artisan for distribution. The film made $248 million from theater sales, giving it the best cost-to-profit ratio ever.

Animated family films also grew in popularity with movies like *Beauty and the Beast* (1991) and *The Lion King* (1994). In 1995, *Toy Story* became the first feature length computer animated film and its success solidified the use of computer animation. At the same time, digital cinema technology began to replace physical film stock.

At the turn of the century, three documentaries appeared and quickly challenged the age-old belief that documentaries would never be main fare: *March of the Penguins* and Michael Moore's *Bowling for Columbine* and *Fahrenheit 9/11* brought this form into the mainstream.

The first decade of the 21st century was truly one of many voices. There were plenty of family movies, like *The Incredibles, Night at the*

Museum, Shrek and its sequels, *Bolt,* and *Monsters, Inc.* Teen movies, such as *Twilight* and its sequels, *Sky High,* and *Shark Boy and Lava Girl* (and sequels) gained in popularity. There was a plethora of kids' movies, animated and not, such as *Ice Age* and its sequels, *Robots,* and *Nanny McPhee.* There was an ongoing stream of blockbusters and sequels, including *The Dark Night, Star Wars,* the entire *Harry Potter* book series, and a continuation of (the apparently endless) James Bond films. There were many innovative, thoughtful movies from independents and majors, such as *Hotel Rwanda, Little Miss Sunshine, Frost/Nixon, Gran Torino, Defiance, Milk, W.,* *No Country for Old Men,* and *Slumdog Millionaire*—which ended up taking eight Oscars. Probably the most controversial movie of the first decade was Mel Gibson's *The Passion of the Christ.* In short, this decade was characterized by excellent films in just about every category, from special effects-focused blockbusters to thought-provoking documentaries. But the struggle of the truly independent filmmaker, the one who has no relationship with a major studio, is not over. There are many films that do not acquire enough funding to complete production and many more that cannot find an outlet for distribution.

The birth and development of the film industry in America has been a story of science, of engineering, of art, and of business. It has been a story of innovation and adaptation; in other words, a constantly changing narrative. But the themes continue and repeat in the present day. The leitmotif is an ongoing conflict between mass-market appeal and the needs of a specialty market, or a conflict between major studios and independent filmmakers. Both are necessary. Mass-market movies entertain many people, help the economy, and provide jobs. Films geared to smaller markets allow for more experimentation and greater individual artistic expression. The best times in the history of film have been when these two come together, as they have in many great movies.

A Brief Chronology

1878: First motion picture, *Sallie Gardner* by Eadweard Mybridge.
1893: First time people pay to see film, at Zoopraxographical Hall; William Kennedy Laurie Dickson invents celluloid strip; the kinetograph and kinetoscope are introduced at the Chicago World's Fair.
1895: Robert W. Paul invents projector and movies are shown to groups for the first time.

1901: First use of flashbacks in dream sequences.

1905: The Nickelodeon, first permanent theater for film only, opens in Pittsburgh; Edwin S. Porter develops single frame animation.

1906: Albert E. Smith and J. Stuart Blackton introduce frame-to-frame animation; the use of arc lights becomes widespread.

1907: First use of cross cutting.

1908: Motion Picture Patents Company formed in the United States; Film d'Art formed in France; the increasing use of intertitles with dialogue.

1910: Filmmakers begin to talk more about their work as "art"; the point of view shot is used; films begin to be divided into divisions of stage, such as drama and comedy.

1911: First use of reverse angle cutting.

1912: Actors begin to receive screen credit; the use of the insert shot to create symbolism grows.

1913: D. W. Griffith starts to direct actors to display emotions; American filmmaking begins the shift from New York to California.

1915: Studio lighting is used for backlighting; *Birth of a Nation* by Griffith.

1918: Denés Mihály invents sound-film.

1927: First use of synchronized sound and dialogue in *The Jazz Singer*.

1929: First adaptation of a musical, *Broadway Melody*.

1934: Leni Riefenstahl's *Triumph des Willens*.

1937: Premier of *Snow White and the Seven Dwarfs*, the first of Disney's animated classics.

1939: *The Wizard of Oz* and *Gone with the Wind*.

1941: *The Maltese Falcon* and *Citizen Kane*.

1942: *Yankee Doodle Dandy* and *Casablanca*.

1943: *Why We Fight* reflects Hollywood's production of wartime propaganda films; *Watch on the Rhine*, an anti-Nazi film.

1946: *It's a Wonderful Life*.

1947: The House Un-American Activities Committee begins its assault on Hollywood seeking to prove that the Screen Writers Guild is a communist organization and that writers and directors are inserting communist propaganda in films; the "Hollywood Ten" refuse to name names.

1950: *Cinderella* is the first of a spate of Disney classics produced in the 1950s; the success of *Rashomon* reflects the increasing worldwide interest in Japanese cinema.

1953: *The Robe* is an example of the type of epic Hollywood is starting to produce in an effort to compete with the increasing use of television.

1955: *The Blackboard Jungle*, one of the first films about the civil rights movement; *To Kill a Mockingbird*, another reflection of the civil rights movement.

1964: Stanley Kubrick's *Dr. Strangelove*, the first commercially successful political satire about nuclear war.

1965: *The Sound of Music* shows that Hollywood is still entertaining audiences with family movies.

1966: *Black Girl* by Ousmane Sembene, the first feature film from an African (Senegalese) filmmaker to get international attention and acclaim.

1968: John Cassavetes' independent film, *Faces*, nominated for three Academy Awards.

1969: Dennis Hopper's *Easy Rider* is an example of the "New-anti-establishment-Hollywood" and the social revolution in the United States.

1971: Kubrick's *A Clockwork Orange*, a violent film about a charismatic psychopath, reflects the beginning of the "New Hollywood," where there is more violence, more sex, and more ambiguity with regard to good and evil; *The French Connection* is the first "R" rated film since the advent of the MPAA rating system to win an Academy Award for Best Picture.

1972: Francis Ford Coppola's *Godfather* trilogy begins and further blurs the lines between good and evil.

1975: Steven Spielberg's *Jaws* breaks box office records.

1978: First Sundance Film Festival.

1979: Coppola's *Apocalypse Now*, which faced so many production delays it was nicknamed "Apocalypse When," is finally released.

1980: Michael Cimino's *Heaven's Gate* flops and brings an end to the auteur-director period and causes studios to take greater control of productions.

1986: *Room with a View* introduces Merchant Ivory to the American public; Oliver Stone speaks out against the Vietnam War with *Platoon*.

1987: *Wall Street*.

1989: *Born on the Fourth of July*; Steven Soderbergh's *Sex, Lies, and Videotape*.

1991: Stone's *JFK*.

1993: *Philadelphia* uses a commercial vehicle with a likeable star, Tom Hanks, to challenge discrimination against people with AIDS; *Schindler's List* brings Spielberg Best Director Academy Award.

1995: *Toy Story*, the first full-length feature done completely with computer animation.

1999: *The Blair Witch Project.*

2000: Ang Lee's *Crouching Tiger, Hidden Dragon*, a martial arts film, is co-produced in China, Hong Kong, Taiwan, and the United States, and becomes the highest-grossing foreign language film in American film history.

2001: DreamWorks' *Shrek.*

2002: Michael Moore's *Bowling for Columbine* becomes the first documentary to compete in the Cannes Film Festival's main competition in 46 years and the highest grossing documentary of all time.

2004: *Fahrenheit 9/11* is the first documentary to win Palme d'Or at Cannes and surpasses *Columbine* at the box office.

2005: *March of the Penguins*, a French nature documentary, wins an Academy Award for Best Documentary; *Brokeback Mountain*, directed by Ang Lee, is an American box office success.

2006: Stone's *World Trade Center; An Inconvenient Truth*, Al Gore's documentary on global warming.

2008: *The Dark Knight's* first weekend breaks all box office records.

2009: *Harry Potter and the Half-Blood Prince* makes the Harry Potter franchise the highest grossing film series of all time.

Chapter 2

State of the Industry

The Hollywood-based film industry has predicted its own demise many times over the past century, but to paraphrase Mark Twain, "Reports of its death have been greatly exaggerated." Each time, rather than being put out of business by new technology, such as television or home video, the industry adapted, evolved, and emerged stronger than ever. Meanwhile independent filmmakers have eagerly awaited each new technological development, hoping it would offer them a way to produce and distribute their films cost effectively and free of the constraints of the major studios. Although digitization and Internet distribution vehicles offer hope, how much opportunity there will be for new voices remains to be seen.

The challenges to the film industry may look different than they did in the past, but the industry is successfully responding the way it has throughout history. Current trends include the banding together of the majors to close doors to outsiders (like Edison's Motion Picture Patent Company did almost 100 years ago), figuring out ways to take over new technology (as it did in the 1950s with television and later with cable and home video), reducing financial risks by encouraging outside investors (as it has since the 1930s), making fewer but bigger movies (as it has since the 1950s), and increased globalization.

Today, film is a global industry even though its headquarters remains in Hollywood. Most production is done not on studio lots (these are used primarily for television now), but "on location" in different states and in different countries. In fact, governments vie for the business generated by location shooting and offer incentives to producers, such

Everyone
Knows
The Film Festivals

Independent producers show their films at festivals hoping to interest a distributor, attract financing from an entertainment banker or private investor, and maybe get some publicity. Distributors—both independent and the majors—go looking to purchase distribution rights to films they think might be profitable. Studio executives go looking for the next young Spielberg. Hopefully, deals will be made. At the very least, contacts will be made.

The Edinburgh International Film Festival, founded in 1947, is the longest continually running festival in the world. The first festival in the United States was the Columbus International Film and Video Festival (also known as the Chris Awards), founded in 1953.

Tops for Independent Films

- Sundance Film Festival
- Tribeca Film Festival
- Ann Arbor Film Festival (experimental films)

The most significant international festivals are accredited by the International Federation of Film Producers Association, or Federation Internationale des Associations de Producteurs de Films

as tax advantages. Distribution is global, and half or more of the revenue from American films comes from abroad. Financing is also global, with foreign governments and individual investors taking part in American productions. There are also more joint productions involving different countries. All this means that people working in the film industry today have to understand and be able to work with people of different cultures. Fluency in another language is also helpful.

But globalization carries its problems along with its benefits. Currently, it is estimated that the movie industry is losing over $6 billion in sales each year due to film piracy, most of it in China. Piracy—the theft of copyrighted motion pictures—is one of the biggest problems facing the motion picture industry and its workers today. It

(FIAPF), which is based in Paris and has member associations throughout the world. The FIAPF lists 13 of the 52 festivals it accredits as "A" festivals, or Category 1 festivals.

The "A" Festivals
- The Cannes Film Festival (le Festival de Cannes)
- The Venice Film Festival
- The Toronto International Film Festival (TIFF)
- The Berlin International Film Festival (also known as Berlinale)
- The Shanghai International Film Festival
- The Moscow International Film Festival (MIFF)
- The San Sebastian International Film Festival (Spain)
- The Montreal World Film Festival (Festival des Films du Monde)
- Locarno International Film Festival (Switzerland)
- The Karlovy Vary International Film Festival (Czech Republic)
- The Mar del Plata Film Festival (Argentina)
- The Cairo International Film Festival (established in 1976 as the first film festival in the Middle East)
- The Tokyo International Film Festival

impacts the studio because nowadays most revenue comes from the post-theatrical release markets—DVD, television, and so on. Even the theatrical market is impacted by piracy when criminals make DVDs available immediately after a movie opens, encouraging people to opt for a cheap DVD and save the price of a ticket. According to the Screen Actors Guild (SAG), piracy also threatens the livelihood of "tens of thousands of actors and others employed by the entertainment industry." These actors, with an average annual salary of $24,000, often survive between jobs with the money they receive from residuals. There are no residuals from pirated material. In 2009, 25 of the 26 movies nominated for an Academy Award (any category) were available online by nomination day. There are clear federal and international laws protecting copyright. The Copyright Act of 1976 outlined copyright infringements; an amendment in 1982 increased penalties and made even first offenses felony crimes. The Communications Act of 1984 and subsequent amendments provided penalties for cable TV and satellite services theft, and the Digital Millennium Copyright Act of 1998 prohibited the circumvention of technological measures use to protect materials. Film copyright is also protected internationally by the Berne Copyright Convention and the World Trade Organization.

Although the studios and unions are united in their efforts to prevent piracy, they are at odds in other legislative endeavors. SAG strongly supports the Employee Free Choice Act, which, it believes, will increase opportunities for workers to organize and lead to more union productions. Similarly, SAG and other unions believe that more independent companies would offer more employment opportunities. But the parent companies of the major studios clearly do not support pending legislation that would limit the number of media companies owned by a single employer.

The Structure of the Film Industry

Companies in the film industry deal with production, distribution, and/or exhibition. Films are made by the production companies, which encompass everything from scripting, shooting, and editing through completion of a master print. Studios and independent producers comprise the production arm. Distributors handle the licensing or sale of prints for theaters, home use (DVDs, videos), television (broadcast or cable), or online use. They deal with both domestic and international distribution. The mega-corporations, which own the major studios, also own distribution companies, and there are independent distribution companies as well. Exhibition includes the retail establishments that actually show or sell the film—domestic and foreign theaters; stores such as Blockbuster, Target, and Walmart; and broadcasters (pay and free television networks).

Production: The "Majors" and the "Indies"

The six main studios, generally referred to as the "studios" or the "majors"—Warner Bros., Universal Pictures, Paramount Pictures, Walt Disney Pictures, 20th Century Fox Films, and Sony Pictures—generate about 90 percent of industry revenue. According to Greenwald and Landry in *This Business of Film*, the majors compete with each other, but they effectively band together to keep others out and to "control standards on technology and pricing, lobbying the government on piracy, and other industry-wide issues."

It is expensive for a studio to produce a film. Although creative talent is contracted on a project basis, studios have huge staffs to cover administrative functions, legal affairs, marketing, publicity, development, production, and distribution. They also have large physical facilities. These items count as overhead and are charged at about 15 percent of the budget for each production. In addition, studio productions use only union talent. The average cost of a studio film in 2007 was about $71 million and big budget films cost upwards of $200 million.

There are many other production companies that partner with the major studios, such as Jerry Bruckheimer at Disney, Imagine at Universal, and Revolution with Sony. These production companies usually fund story acquisition and script development while the studio covers the major production costs. The production company then receives a fee and a percentage of profits. Some independent production companies are able to finance their own projects and engage with a studio only for distribution and sometimes for a modest amount of additional financing.

While the majors tend to look toward potential *tent pole* movies— big budget, heavily promoted films (such as blockbuster sequels) that are expected to quickly reap a huge profit and "hold up the studio tent"—to cover their high overhead, the smaller companies often focus on medium-risk, medium-upside movies. How difficult it is to compete or even survive as an independent entity is illustrated by the saga of DreamWorks SKG, the studio formed by Steven Spielberg, Jeffrey Katzenberg, and David Geffen in 1994. By 2006, this triumvirate realized it could not compete with the majors and sold DreamWorks to Paramount. In 2009 Spielberg and his producing executive Stacey Snider broke away from Paramount and, maintaining the DreamWorks name, began seeking funding for another independent company. As evidence of the global trend, two of the investors include India's Reliance ADA Group and the Israel Discount Bank. According to *BusinessWeek*, another investor, Disney, has agreed to distribute at least six DreamWorks's films.

Truly independent small companies and individual independent filmmakers who have no connection to any studio generally produce films with very low budgets, usually under $5 million.

Improvements in the quality of videotape have lowered costs and increased opportunities for individual producers. Digital editing and special effects also make it possible for individuals to produce movies with a much lower budget. So while the majors focus on mass-market, box office bonanzas to cover their costs, the independent or somewhat independent companies produce less expensive films that appeal to a smaller audience. This has led to a wide range of offerings, from special-effects blockbusters to romantic comedies, intellectual or artistic films, and documentaries.

Non-Theatrical Production: The Industrials

There are many small production companies that address the non-theatrical market. They produce programs for specialized audiences. There are companies that produce medical education programs for physicians and other health workers. These programs are generally shown in hospitals. There are companies that produce programs for corporations, usually addressing employee training. These programs often include role-playing vignettes to show employees "right" and "wrong" ways to handle difficult customer issues. The industry also serves corporations and nonprofit foundations by producing films that publicize their work and that may be used for fund-raising. Some of these programs are distributed via the Internet or appear on the corporation's Web site. Many people enter the field by working for one of these companies. Since these industrial production companies have small staffs with less-defined functions, new employees get varied experience and can move up quickly, developing skills and experience to help them get a job in theatrical productions.

Distribution: The "Megas" and the "Majors"

The all-powerful majors are in reality only small parts of their "mega" parent companies. These parent companies all have distribution arms to handle licensing and sales to theater chains, television, cable, DVD, and so on. "Since the studios are a low-margin business," explains RBC Capital Markets analyst David Bank in a 2009 *BusinessWeek* article, "the conglomerates that own them look beyond a film's box-office results for additional revenues from DVD sales to video-on-demand to licensing of characters and concepts to toy and video game merchandisers." What follows is a brief overview of the relationship between key majors and their parent companies:

➡ Warner Bros. is owned by Time Warner, Inc., the largest media company, which has interests in publishing, the Internet, music, and cable. Warner Bros. films are distributed by a multitude of Warner and New Line labels, such as Warner Bros. Pictures, Warner Bros. Pictures International, and New Line Distribution. Warner Bros. opened a distribution and marketing operation in China with China Audio Video and also has a partnership with Abu Dhabi Media Company.

➡ Universal is owned by General Electric, which also owns NBC and the cable interests of Vivendi. Universal distributors include Universal Pictures, Focus Features, Rogue Pictures, and others.

➡ Paramount is owned by Viacom, which is owned by National Amusements, and owns CBS and other media companies. Distributors include Paramount Pictures, Paramount Vantage, and others.

➡ Disney is owned by the Walt Disney Company, which owns ABC as well as the famed theme parks and merchandisers. Distributors include Buena Vista, Hollywood Pictures, Touchstone, Miramax, Pixar, and others.

➡ Twentieth Century Fox is owned by News Corporation, which owns music, cable, and publishing companies. Distributor divisions include 20th Century Fox, Fox Searchlight, and others.

➡ Sony Studios is, of course, part of Sony Corporation with its enormous electronics business. Distributors include Sony Pictures Releasing, Sony Screen Gems, Sony Picture Classics, and Columbia TriStar.

There are also independent distribution companies not owned by a major studio. These companies distribute films geared to more limited audiences. They tend to release their movies theatrically in just a few cities and then expand if the film generates a favorable response. Independent distributors include Magnolia Releasing, Zeitgeist Film, and Palm Pictures. Some of the independent production companies, such as Lionsgate and Summit Entertainment, have their own distribution arms.

A huge cost savings in distribution has recently been made possible by technology that allows the distributor to electronically transmit a digital print to a theater rather than having to reproduce and

---

INTERVIEW

The Film Industry: Now and Tomorrow

Howard Weinberg
Award-winning documentary filmmaker, television journalist, and educator
New York, New York

What are you currently working on?

I'm co-teaching a new documentary seminar at Columbia University's Graduate School of Journalism, and I am currently working on a documentary about the TV LAB, an innovative period in public television from 1972 to 1984 (see Howardweinberg.net). I also help other documentary filmmakers improve their films as a script doctor (see Script-doctor.net).

How would you assess the current state of the film industry in this country?

The major motion picture industry is in great shape. States are catering to Hollywood to try to attract location filming. They are offering all sorts of tax rebates and discounted services. State film commissions are clamoring for their business. Things are still difficult for the small independents, the ones not associated with a studio or major company, but that may improve with the new technology. The opportunity to promote something on the Web, to create a fan base, to distribute on the Web by purchasing DVDs or downloads has never been greater.

What new technology is influencing the industry at this time?

Technology is constantly changing. Right now we are in the midst of a technology merger, a merger of the computer and the television set. You can already download full-length features on to your computer or another electronic device. In a short time the process to project downloaded films on to your big screen television will be perfected and more widely available. The issue then becomes how to adjust the business model, how to make money from Internet distribution.

How does new or relatively new technology impact production and distribution costs?

Some developments have made production much less expensive. People can emulate film quality digitally and without the scratches. You can now get high definition video with a contrast ratio comparable to film. When people watched the Danish film, *The Celebration*, the first feature shot entirely on video, they could not tell the difference. George Lucas shot his recent *Star Wars* movies on video. Nowadays people do not even pay attention to whether it is shot on film or video, and that creates a great cost savings. The real issue in how the picture looks is not whether it is shot on film or video but how it was lit. Distribution has been made cheaper and easier now that we can transfer digital prints electronically to theaters rather than sending cans of film.

So production and distribution costs are now lower. Are there other costs independent filmmakers need to think about?
There are many. For example, you may need to purchase music and stock footage rights. There was a film called *Tarnation* that cost $218 to produce and $400,000 to clear music and clip rights. There are many more costs to make a film ready for theatrical distribution, but these can usually be picked up by the distributor once you have one who believes in your product. For example, *The Blair Witch Project* was initially made for under $30,000. But it cost an additional half-million dollars or more to get the sound and picture quality suitable for distribution.

It sounds like getting a good distributor is essential?
At this point it is really important. It can take a year or more for a good film to find a distributor. The distributor needs to get behind your film, to identify your film's target audience, and to market it to that audience. There's a lot of product out there. Sometimes the distributor will have to spend as much on advertising and promotion as the filmmaker spent on production. Imagine trying to get a low budget independent film noticed when the studios spend an average of $40 million on the marketing, promotion, and advertising of each film! You want a distributor who will know how to reach your film's target audience. Documentary filmmaker Alex Gibney sued his distributor for allegedly failing to adequately publicize and distribute his controversial film, *Taxi to the Darkside*.

How do you go about getting a distributor?
Most independents try to catch the eye of a distributor by showing their films at festivals. It's not easy. You might not get your film into the festivals you want or a festival may charge you a lot of money and give you a terrible time slot. When I made *Sid at 90*, we got it into 30 festivals across the country, but not into Boston where many of Sid's relatives lived. There is an art to playing the festivals to maximize your chances. Some movies demand special attention. After Hol-

(continues on next page)

INTERVIEW

The Film Industry: Now and Tomorrow (continued)

lywood didn't quite know what to do with *Bonnie and Clyde*, actor/producer Warren Beatty got it re-released, found critics to praise it, took the film to smaller cities to get noticed, and then parlayed that enthusiasm across America until it became one of the defining films of the 1960s.

As with everything in life, timing plays an important role in whether or not an independent film makes it. The timing was right for *Juno, Little Miss Sunshine*, and *Supersize Me*, films that could have taken much longer to be picked up had they not reflected major issues of the time. *Supersize Me* was released while there was a lawsuit against McDonald's.

Do you see this changing in the near future?
It is already changing somewhat. There are Web sites like Indiepix-

ship the film. The cost savings realized by digital transmission has been a great boon to IMAX. The majors were hesitant to use IMAX because of high distribution costs and limited theatrical outlets. According to Warner Bros., a single IMAX film print ran $60,000 compared to $1,000 for a standard print. That is because the IMAX motion picture format uses larger film stock and six-channel audio to enhance picture and sound quality. As Brooks Barnes reports in a 2009 *New York Times* article, IMAX was able to sharply reduce distribution costs to just $500 a print by switching to digital prints. In addition, IMAX has reached beyond museums and science centers and now operates more than 250 commercial theaters.

Distribution: Internet Protocol Television (IPTV)

The film industry has not yet figured out how it will be impacted by Internet Protocol Television (IPTV) as this technology becomes more sophisticated and overcomes certain barriers. Currently, movies can films.com, Hulu.com, and Snagfilms.com where you can either download a film and pay to view it, or view it for free, or buy a DVD, or even put a film on your own Web site. Another startup, Indiegogo. com, offers tools for independents to fundraise, promote, and distribute their films online. A lot of independents make trailers for downloadable sites and then charge for the viewing of the full film, or they give away their film for free and make money selling DVDs.

What advice would you give to people who are starting out, people who are near the beginning of their careers?
If possible I would urge them to start out in a large studio or production company, even if it is in a very menial job. This way you can get an overview of the entire process. You'll see all the jobs, what all the people do. Ideally, your next job should be with a smaller group where you can do more hands-on work, make mistakes, and maybe even apprentice yourself to someone who will teach you a little during quieter moments. Show initiative but do not become annoying, do not demand that people pay attention to you. We once had an intern who traveled with us to several locations in one day. He asked so many questions that by the end of the day people were running away from him. You have to find that middle ground between letting people know you have initiative and want to learn and not irritating them.

be transmitted to the home through IPTV via streaming or downloading. Streaming offers more protection against copying because the movie is transmitted to the computer's hard drive in sections as the viewer watches, and then it is destroyed. With downloading, the complete file is sent and therefore more susceptible to piracy. In 2006, global revenues from IPTV were $779.2 million according to analysts at iSuppli Corporation. These analysts project revenues of $26.3 billion by 2011.

There are at least 50 Web sites in the United States where people can view, rent, or download movies. Examples of sites for online viewing include ABC.com, Apple's iTunes, Hulu, Nickelodeon (nick. com), Xbox.com, and Netflix. The major barrier to even more widespread use of IPTV is that most people would rather watch a film on a full-size television set than on the screen of a computer, mobile phone, iPod, or game console. But most believe it is only a matter of time—and not much time, at that—before a cost-effective, easy-to-use method is found to transmit IPTV to a television monitor directly or via a wireless local area network. Some companies are in the process of designing systems that will interface with portable players, which can then network with a television. The Roxio CinemaNow service from Sonic Solutions is available on certain LG electronics and other items. Sonic's goal is to show consumers how easy it is to stream Hollywood hit movies on to their media players, Blu-ray disc players, mobile phones, Web-connected TV sets, and PCs equipped with Roxio Venue software. Technology to eliminate the long download times necessary for a full-length feature without sacrificing video and audio quality is also in development.

From the point of view of the majors, the issue is how to make money with this type of distribution and how to build it without cannibalizing the TV and DVD companies they currently own. From the vantage point of the independents, particularly individual independent filmmakers, the potential is exciting. They look toward the possibility of finally being able to reach an audience without the financing necessary for theatrical or even TV or DVD distribution. But they are trying to figure out how they will promote their movies and make people aware of their films.

Distribution: Dilemmas of the Independents

In spite of technology that has reduced both production and distribution costs, the big problem for the independent (individual) filmmaker is getting his or her film out to the public—getting a distributor to buy the rights to distribute their film. One of the best ways to find a distributor, or have one find you, is to have your film shown at as many festivals as possible. There are many tiers of festivals, ranging from those addressing a niche to the world famous ones, like Cannes.

Le Festival de Cannes is widely viewed as the most influential film festival in the world. The most significant festivals for independent filmmakers include the prestigious Sundance Film Festival and New York City's Tribeca Film Festival. Sundance, held annually in Utah in January, is the largest U.S. festival and focuses on new work from independent filmmakers in the United States and abroad. In 2002, Robert DeNiro and Jane Rosenthal founded the Tribeca festival to aid the recovery of lower Manhattan in the wake of September 11th and to highlight New York City as a film center. The Ann Arbor Film Festival is considered the most important festival for experimental films. There are many smaller niche festivals, such as those focusing on horror films, film noir, or films of a particular region or country. A festival for environmental films opened in 2009 at Yale University. In addition to festivals, filmmakers can try to get financing and a distributor's interest by playing trailers of their films on Web sites such as Indiepics.com.

The script for the independent filmmaker is not yet completed. Digital technology has significantly reduced the cost of both production and distribution. The next major boon to independents will be the ability to transmit their films via the Internet. But that will not solve all their challenges. It will still be necessary to make people aware of a movie, to motivate them to see it, and to figure out a way to recoup some of their costs— and maybe even make a profit.

Exhibition

This is the final phase before counting the money. Where is the film exhibited? Most films begin domestically in theaters, and distributors plan and negotiate with different theater chains. They may test the waters by first distributing to a few theaters, or they may saturate the market and hit nationwide chains simultaneously. Other components of the exhibition phase are not solely involved in motion pictures. There are the retailers for DVDs, such as Blockbuster, Walmart, and Target; the online services; the broadcasters, pay and free; the ancillary exhibitors, such as airlines and cruise companies; and the foreign theaters and broadcasters. Not surprisingly, the megacorporations, which own the studios and several distribution companies, also own many of the exhibition outlets, including theater chains and television networks.

The Filmmaking Process

A studio movie, or a movie produced by one of the larger independents, involves so many departments, so many divisions, so many companies, so many different types of professionals, that even a business veteran can have trouble keeping it all straight. Undoubtedly, there are many in the production realm who have never thought about the accounting and marketing end of the business. Similarly, how many entertainment lawyers really understand the work of a gaffer or a best boy? Anyone who has sat through the credits of a major feature film knows that it took a lot to get the germ of an idea to the theater. The process begins with development and financing.

Professional Ethics

Product Placement

The budget was tight. The producer was afraid they would not be able to finish shooting. Then an agent who liaises between corporations and filmmakers to place products in movies approached him. Not only was a well-known car manufacturer willing to donate three expensive cars for the chase scene they were about to shoot, but it would also pay $200,000. The producer could not believe his good luck—until some additional details of the proposed deal surfaced. The car manufacturer wanted the chase scene shot in a way that would highlight some of the cars' best new features. The automaker also wanted the hero to make some favorable comments about the brand. "Just have the writer weave in how fast this ___ can reach 90 mph."

What should he do? Everyone was doing it. Since sales of Reese's Pieces soared 70 percent after they were eaten in ET, the use of product placement, or embedded advertising, in movies had skyrocketed.

Development and Financing

Only one in ten projects developed by studios is produced, and the ratio is worse for independent producers. However, this is a necessary evil—it is only by methodically going through the development process that one can make a judgment about whether or not to produce a particular film.

Development begins with an idea. The idea is pitched to a studio with a lot of supporting materials. The supporting package has to convince the studio (and ultimately potential investors) that this is a hot property, a movie that will succeed at the box office and make money for everyone. Is it an engrossing story with likeable characters? Does it clearly fit a niche for marketing? Is it visually appealing? Why do you think audiences will flock to see it? "Development hell" refers to what the producer or director goes through as he or she shepherds the property through the studio, changing it, answering questions, gathering more information, until there is finally (possibly) a green light. Sometimes the producer or director bases the package on a script or idea received by a writer. In other cases, the producer

It had history. In 1896 the Lumiére brothers featured Sunshine Soap, a Lever product, in their films. If it was okay for Spielberg and the Lumiére brothers, wasn't it okay for him? Why did he have that knot in his stomach?

As he ruminated, his real views and feelings surfaced. To him, part of the issue was the quality or type of product. He would not want to encourage young people to smoke by associating cigarettes with his hero character. But his film had a chase scene and these cars were no worse than any of their competitors. Part of the issue was how much product placement would be in his film. He would not want his film to look like a montage of ads. Product placement was just another way to help fund a movie—except when it influenced the creative process, or when the director would have to shoot the scene a certain way, or when the writer would have to alter the script.

He had his answer. He negotiated with the agent. He got the cars. He got half the money. And he got to keep his integrity.

contacts a writer once the idea is making its way through the process. The producer might buy the script outright and take a risk if it is not produced; or he or she may "option" the script, meaning that for a fee the producer maintains exclusive rights to it for a discrete period of time. This is a stage that involves writers, director, producers, studio executives, and everyone's advisers—attorneys, agents, and managers. Although many script writers consider themselves underpaid, others do quite well, and purchasing a script without a studio commitment to produce the film can be risky. Sony bought the script for *Evan Almighty* (originally called *Passion of the Ark*) for $2.5 million; *The Sixth Sense* script sold for $3 million in 1999.

What if someone along the way steals the idea before anyone in the public knows about it? To protect against this, the writer or producer registers each step in the process—outline, treatment, script— with the Writers Guild of America. The copyright is automatically secured as soon as the work is created.

A realistic budget is an essential component of the development package, necessary to show to potential investors. The major studios and the large independents, such as Lionsgate and Weinstein, can "raise capital at the corporate level through the public or private equity and debt markets, or by offering investors economic interests in a slate of films," explains Greenwald and Landry. It is much more difficult for independent producers who must obtain financing for each individual film, a far riskier proposition in the eyes of most investors. At this point financial analysts and accountants join the cast of characters involved in deciding whether or not to produce a film.

Whether or not to produce a film is an executive decision based largely on the chance of profitability, but creative team members are involved as well. The writer may be tweaking the treatment or script to reflect concerns of the studio execs. The producer may reach out to actors and directors known to be box office draws.

Preproduction

The devil is in the details during the preproduction phase, and if any details have been overlooked, the wrath of Satan will be felt during the costly and stressful production phase. During this phase all arrangements for filming are made, including casting, location permits, insurance, and scheduling. To be time efficient and cost effective, scenes must be shot according to location and actor roles. If union actors are used, as they will be for all studio productions, actors are paid from their first day of work through their last day, including any nonworking days in between. Hence, it pays—literally—to bunch as much actor time together as possible. Contingency plans are important here. What if it rains during the time scheduled for an outdoor shoot? What if you are shooting a hospital scene on location in a trauma center and there is a car crash? What do you do if you have just finished setup in the trauma room and suddenly ambulances speed in, paramedics push 12 stretchers into the trauma center, and you are blocking everyone with your camera and lights? What if an actor comes down with the flu? The list is endless. No one knows what will go wrong on any given shoot, but everyone knows something will go wrong. Meticulous planning during the preproduction stage includes ways of dealing with possible mishaps. Contingency plans include alternate scenes that can be shot if a particular scene—like that outdoor scene on a rainy day or the trauma scene during an emergency—has to be put off. Contingency plans have to consider which actors are on call, what equipment is being used, and so on. In public places like trauma centers, you need to plan the fastest way to strike the set and get out of the way.

Production

This is when, as they say, the clock is ticking and time is money—a lot of money. Consider everyone who is paid for a wasted day of filming. On a small, industrial production this may be several thousand dollars, but that may be 30 percent of the budget. On a large studio production the costs can be staggering. Production days are long— very long. Tempers flare and everyone feels the stress. Getting the best product and staying on schedule often feel like conflicting aims, yet both are important. While one scene is being shot, someone has to be gathering talent and equipment for the next scene. Union talent has to have breaks and meals on a certain schedule. Someone has to make sure catering is available at the best break times.

Postproduction

Since people have become accustomed to the miracles of digital editing, the phrase "we'll fix it in post" is often heard on the set. In fact, many production flaws can be covered up during a digital edit—many, but certainly not all. Some people shoot film, do initial edits digitally, then physically cut the film, like they did for all films until recently. Now, many people make a digital print, whether they shot film or high-definition video, and complete all editing digitally. With the new technology, it is almost impossible to tell the difference. In a way, digital editing is less stressful than cutting actual film since you never ruin or lose raw material. On the other hand, digital editing usually involves expensive equipment and a team of editors and engineers—in other words, time is money. As in preproduction and production, planning is key.

Marketing and Distribution

Distribution and marketing work hand in hand, ideally from early in the production phase, if not before. Sometimes distributors have a role in financing the production. Distribution has become increasingly challenging and creative as more outlets have opened up. Choosing theater chains has now become just a small part of the picture. Timing domestic and international releases as well as the non-theatrical outlets, such as DVD, pay TV, cable TV, and broadcast are equally important. There once was a formula, a path to follow from domestic theaters to international theaters, to DVD, to pay-per-view TV, to rental. But distributors need to constantly adapt to changes in viewing patterns and technology. They also need to consider timing an opening around events such as the Oscars or other films being released, and they need to consider time of year and people's viewing habits. The distribution arrangements begin early, and marketing is planned from the beginning and initiated prior to the film's premiere with the hope of quickly saturating the market on release. Underneath the creativity, however, there is a lot of detail, a lot of legal paperwork for different licensing agreements, cost analysis, and so on.

The marketing budget usually runs about half of the production cost. That translates into a marketing budget of about $30 million for the average $71 million studio film. Sometimes more money is spent on marketing than on production. The more locations a film simultaneously opens in, the more money needed for national advertising. Marketing includes all the promotion and advertising that will be produced to let the target audience know about a movie, with the goal of making them yearn to see it.

The target audience is identified during the development phase—it is how a particular film idea will be greeted by the target audience that suggests how profitable a movie might be. The marketers and distributors have to make sure the promotional materials, as well as the film itself, get the rating they want for it. You cannot target teenagers with an R-rated film. Sometimes, the producer and distributor collaborate to recut a movie geared to kids and teens if it looks like the original cut will not get a G, PG, or PG-13 rating. Movies are rated by the Classification and Ratings Administration (CARA), under the auspices of the Motion Picture Association of America (MPAA).

A strategy for reaching a target audience is developed and then all materials are built to address this strategy. The goal is to begin to pique interest awhile before release and then build to a crescendo immediately before release, resulting in the highest possible box office sales during the movie's opening weekend. For some films, saturating toy stores with action figures prior to release is another marketing tool.

The Impact of the Motion Picture Industry on the U.S. Economy

The film industry has been a major force supporting the U.S. economy for decades. As of 2009, the motion picture and television industry employed 2.5 million Americans in a wide range of professions and trades; it involved 115,000 businesses spread across all 50 states; it helped support the infrastructure of many American cities; and it was one of the top American exporters, boasting a $13.6 billion trade surplus. (Statistics in this subsection are from a Motion Picture Association of America 2009 report, "The Economic Impact of the Motion Picture and Television Industry on the United States.")

The 2.5 million jobs provided by the industry include 285,000 people—full time, part time, and freelance—directly involved in the business of making, distributing, and marketing motion pictures and television shows. While many work for the majors or for independent production or distribution companies, others work for companies that supply the film industry, such as film labs, special effects and animation studios, casting companies, agents, wardrobe, and prop companies. According to the Motion Picture Industry Association of America (MPAA), "The industry employs workers in every major occupational group, including actors, accountant, agents, animators, camera operators, casting directors, computer specialists, directors, editors, engineers, graphic designers, marketers, producers, special effects technicians, writers, and many, many more." There are 478,000 more people employed by related businesses, such as movie theaters, video rental operations, and cable and broadcast TV companies. Finally, about 1.7 million people are in jobs that indirectly support the industry, such as car rental dealers, caterers, lumber suppliers, and truckers. The MPAA reports that the average salary for production employees is almost $75,000, 26 percent higher than the national average salary.

Although everyone associates the film industry with Hollywood and, to a lesser extent, New York, it provides jobs and supports businesses in every state. Of the 115,000 companies making up the motion picture industry, 81 percent employ fewer than 10 people. This figure comprises companies involved in the full-time making and distribution of films and TV shows. It does not include businesses that supply other industries as well as the film industry, such as caterers, florists, and truckers.

States vie for location productions because of the many ways in which they help the state's economy, from providing jobs for local individuals and small businesses, to building infrastructure, to generating tax revenue. In 2007, sales taxes and taxes paid by workers generated about $4.1 billion in federal revenue, $1.9 billion in state taxes, and $6.4 billion in unemployment.

Finally, while many U.S. consumers opt for cars and technology from Japan and consumer goods from China and Korea, year after year

On the Cutting Edge

Studios Set the Stage for Globalization

Everyone talks about globalization, about the worldwide reach of corporations. The film industry leads the way. Every aspect of the film industry is global, from generating financing, to adjusting a script to maximize global appeal, to arranging licensing agreements in foreign markets, to working on co-productions. The Noci Pictures Entertainment Web site promotes a "one-stop global film finance and production service consulting division." Noci puts the film producer or studio in touch with possible financiers, many of them foreign, and helps them structure investment agreements. According to Mike Goodridge (reporting at Screendaily.com), in 2004 Warner Bros. Pictures formed the first joint venture film company with China, Warner ChinaFilm Hg Corporation, in partnership with China Film Group and Hengdian Group. In June 2009 Amaru, a broadband media entertainment company, announced that its subsidiary M2B World Asia Pacific (M2B) entered into an agreement with Beijing Baidu Netcome Science and Technology, a subsidiary of a Chinese language Internet search provider. M2B anticipates that this partnership will allow it to reach the fast-growing online video and advertising markets in China, according to My Techbox Online. In a 2008 report, the China Internet Network Information Center reported that there were about 180 million online video users in mainland China.

Many countries have film commissions associated with the Association of Film Commissioners International (AFCI). These commissions offer incentives to U.S. production companies in the form of grants, interest free loans, and tax incentives. They also facilitate production arrangements. Canada leads the way in attracting U.S. productions (with New York City street scenes often filmed in Toronto), but there are active film commissions in many countries, including Ireland, Italy, Hong Kong, Austria, South Africa, Australia, France, Germany, and Jamaica.

the film industry generates a positive balance of trade, $13.6 billion in 2007. It also contributes to national self-esteem—American films are considered the gold standard to which others compare themselves.

As of 2009, the top 10 production states, excluding California and New York, were Illinois, Texas, Florida, Georgia, Pennsylvania, New Jersey, North Carolina, Louisiana, Tennessee, and Massachusetts. Coming close and rapidly rising are Michigan, Arizona, Connecticut, New Mexico, and Utah. In 2007, as Michigan's primary industry was crumbling and scores of auto workers were being laid off, Clint Eastwood's *Gran Torino* and the TV show *Prayers for Bobby* paid $523.9 million in local wages. In her 2008 State of the State speech, Governor Jennifer Granholm called for an aggressive film incentive. The tax incentives offered to motion picture studios were designed not just to attract individual productions, but also to provide for permanent job growth. In fact, Michigan's success in attracting location shooting is expected to create 5,993 new jobs, including 4,066 film, animation, and programming jobs. But that is not all. Two major infrastructure projects are underway: An $85.9 million venture, Detroit Center Studios, will produce visual effects and animation; and Motown Motion Pictures in Pontiac, a $70 million investment, will include a film studio, a production company, and nine sound stages.

Michigan is not the only state benefiting from the film industry's investment in infrastructure. A multimillion dollar film and TV studio, Tyler Perry Studios, opened in Atlanta in 2008; Norristown Studios in Norristown, Pennsylvania, opened in 2009; a new studio on a campus in West Palm Beach, Florida, opened in 2009; and a $10 million production and postproduction facility opened in Anchorage, Alaska, in 2009. Some projects currently under construction include Celtic Media Centre, a $45 million venture in Baton Rouge; Spiderwood Studios in Bastrop, Texas; a soundstage and studio in Wilmington, North Carolina; a studio in Shreveport, Louisiana; and a new studio with a theater, offices, and a hotel in Plymouth, Massachusetts. Plans are underway to build Kapolei studios in Oahu, Hawaii, which will include four sound stages, offices, dressing rooms, set construction and production spaces, a student film annex, and a backlot with sets and retailers. A new studio in Sante Fe, New Mexico, is also in the planning stages. It will include 10 sound stages. Several other projects are, of course, underway in California and New York. In California, Technicolor, Inc., put up a six-story building for postproduction in Los Angeles; Sony Pictures Entertainment erected two more buildings on its Culver City lot; and Commonwealth Studios broke ground for a $125 million studio in Moorpark. In New York, the Museum of the Moving Image in

Astoria broke ground for an extension, and the Jacob Burns Film Center in Pleasantville opened a new Media Arts Lab.

Recent films have done great things for the economy of most if not all states. In just two months of shooting and several more before and after in prep and wrap up, *Leatherheads* paid over $1.7 million to local cast, extras, crew, and other employees in South Carolina and $2.3 million in North Carolina. The movie also employed 4,720 local residents in South Carolina and 6,745 in North Carolina, and paid almost $3 million to local businesses, such as hardware stores, hotels, dry cleaners, and caterers in South Carolina and almost $2.5 million to businesses in North Carolina. Everyone knows that the film industry is a major contributor to the California economy, but the amount is still staggering. *Angels and Demons* used a team of over 450 visual-effects illustrators and technicians to recreate St. Peter's Basilica and other Italian landmarks at the studio. It took 272 construction workers to build sets that looked like the Vatican and other sites in Rome. During two years of production, the movie employed 1,400 people, including 1,000 union technicians. *Marley and Me* provided employment for more than just humans in Florida and Pennsylvania. Twenty-two dogs were used to play Marley, including several shelter dogs that were adopted following production. The Association of Pet Dog Trainers used the film to promote dog training and qualified trainers. The film hired 2,500 local cast and crew members and used local vendors for soundproofing and building sets.

Here is what some mayors and governors have written about the impact of production on their states:

➜ "When Warner Bros. filmed *The Dark Knight* in Chicago, it generated a record $40 million in revenue, employed more than 4,000 people, and purchased goods and services from over 300 members."—Mayor Richard M. Daley, Chicago

➜ "In these challenging and uncertain times for the economy the creation of movies and television programs can potentially be a bright star on the horizon for the Commonwealth."—Governor Steve Beshear, Kentucky

➜ "For more than 50 years, we have seen economic benefits flow to our workforce and especially to the small businesses serving the industry...[I] will do everything I can to preserve this essential part of Texas' economy."—Governor Rick Perry, Texas

→ "More than 100,000 local New Yorkers rely on the behind-the-scenes jobs that are created when film and television productions shoot in our city...film and television industry generates about $5 billion each year in local economic activity, making it one of our most important —and exciting—industries."—Mayor Michael R. Bloomberg, New York

→ "The motion picture and television industry helps drive California's diverse economy, employing over 200,000 Californian and generating more than $35 billion in economic activity."—Governor Arnold Schwarzenegger, California

As if jobs, support of small businesses, tax revenue, and infrastructure support were not enough, location filming is the gift that keeps on giving. According to a study published in the *Journal of Travel Research*, "A location featured in a successful film can see an increase of up to 75 percent in tourism the year after the film is released." Sometimes places continue to attract tourists many years after a film is produced. You would not consider Dyersville, Iowa, a hot spot of tourism, but the town gets 65,000 tourists a year to visit the cornfield photographed in the 20-year-old film, *Field of Dreams*. The New Mexico Tourism Department reported that film-related tourism represented 5.5 percent of total tourism expenditures after the release of *No Country for Old Men* and *3:10 to Yuma*. Tourism in some Alaskan locations rose 100 percent after *Into the Wild*. *Nights in Rodanthe* dramatically increased tourism to the Outer Banks of North Carolina, according to the Visitors Bureau there. Film companies and tourism organizations often plan campaigns to increase tourism. For example, the Santa Barbara Conference and Visitors Bureau offered vineyard visitors a map of locations from the film *Sideways*. There was a 300 percent increase of visitors to several wineries the year after the film was released.

Another side-benefit to the film industry is, like NASA, the technology the film industry has developed for its own use has contributed to the progress of science and service of humanity. Some examples include development of environmentally friendly fireworks; facial recognition and biometric scanning; crash barriers to protect buildings from vehicle intrusion; fasteners to make mechanical structures safer, such as planes, bridges, and roller coasters; and passenger restraint systems.

Employment Opportunities

Through good economic times and bad the movie industry has prospered. According to the Bureau of Labor Statistics, the industry will continue to grow because of "the explosive increase in demand for programming needed to fill the rising number of cable and satellite television channels both in the United States and abroad." The industry provides career opportunities for the broadest range of people, from accountants, lawyers, publicists, and marketing executives, to actors, directors, and producers. Although competition for top jobs in acting, producing, directing, and writing will always be keen, there are numerous other opportunities in both the creative and business ends of the industry. Some of the best job prospects are for multimedia artists and animators, editors, people skilled in computer-generated effects, sound engineers, and set construction workers and other craftspeople.

Representing the fastest growing sector, as of 2009 over 10,000 artists and engineers were working in the industry, and that number is expected to grow by 25 percent. Constantly changing technology makes the work of artists and computer engineers who work on special effects and animation particularly challenging and exciting. They are frequently confronted with an "impossible" task. For example, when production began on *Spider-Man 3* there were no computer programs that could create the effects the director wanted. So Sony artists and engineers wrote original code to create a character made entirely of sand. The visual effects team at Blue Sky Studios often has to write custom software tools to create desired effects, such as exploding lava geysers or falling snow in the *Ice Age* films.

There is a need for almost every occupation in the film industry, whether for staff employment with studios, independent producers, or distributors; for one of the companies that work with the studios, such as small production companies, casting companies, equipment suppliers, costume designers, and makeup artists; or for contract (project) work for a studio or for one of its suppliers. Although Los Angeles is still the hub of the industry, there are many local employers that provide staff and services when a film is shot on location.

It is not surprising that the film industry employs a disproportionate number of people under 34. Jobs involved in production usually involve long hours and a lot of travel. Jobs on the business end—in accounting, marketing, or legal for example—may be similar to comparable positions in other industries. Also, while through-the-roof compensation is paid to star actors and directors, other salaries can be quite low. Consequently, people who do not move up in a reasonable amount of time often move to another field. Although the MPAA survey reported an average salary of $75,000 for those in production jobs, it is important to note that the salary range in all phases of the industry is wide. Salaries or per diems, since most jobs are on a project-by-project basis, are generally very low if you are in an entry level or near entry level position. Those who can afford it sometimes work in unpaid internships, even after graduation. At the other end are the astronomical salaries of star actors, directors, and writers. The salaries of those in the middle—beyond entry level and below star—depend largely on whether or not the person belongs to a union. However, even union salaries differ based on the type of production. For instance, the Director's Guild of America (DGA) divides salaries according to the budget of the motion picture. According to the DGA, the recommended weekly salary for a director in 2009–2010 is $15,637, and that will jump to $46,184 in 2010–2011. But if the motion picture is low budget, the weekly salary can be $13,000 to $14,000. Similarly, a unit production manager weekly salary of $4,313 drops to $1,423 for a low budget production; the first assistant director salary of $4,100 per week is $1,353 on a low budget film; the second assistant director salary of $2,594 is $625 on a low budget movie.

When looking at daily or weekly salaries, it is important to remember that most people do not work every day. The current Screen Actor's Guild minimum daily rate for a union actor is $759, but SAG reports that fewer than 5 percent of its members earn their living from full-time acting and the average annual actor salary is $24,000 a year. The current Writer's Guild of America agreement ranges from $58,477 to $109,783 for an original screenplay. While non-union writers get much less, coveted writers with a history of success can earn several million for one script. The Bureau of Labor Statistics reported that the median hourly earnings in May 2006 were $25.76 for film and video editors, $21.16 for camera operators, $16.60 for audio and video equipment technicians, and $10.69 for actors.

Unions and Professional Associations

From the early days of film through the Golden Age of Hollywood, most people in the industry were employees of the studios, and most were not treated well. Unions sprung up between the 1930s and 1950s to protect actors, writers, directors, and others. The unions strove for decent pay and working conditions.

The unions associated with the film business are of value to both the union member and the studio. Union members are protected by regulations regarding pay, overtime, and hours worked. Since most work is on a project or contract basis, industry workers receive their medical and other benefits from their union. The studio or production company benefits because union members must meet certain minimum requirements in their field and adhere to the guidelines of the union.

The studios and major production companies can use only union talent. This makes their productions more costly. However, since union members are not permitted to work on nonunion productions, producers who do not use union talent are limited in their choices. Some of the unions allow members to join a category called "financial core" in which they can accept union and nonunion employment but cannot vote or run for office in the union. Since most work in the business is contract or project work, union agreements are negotiated between the individual union or guild and the Alliance of Motion Picture and TV Producers (AMPTP), representing the major studios.

The film industry has been shut down by union strikes several times. There were Writers Guild Strikes in 1998 (22 weeks) and 2007–2008 (three months). Members of the Screen Actors Guild went on strike for three months in 1980 and for six months in 2000.

The primary unions, guilds, and professional associations in the film industry are:

→ **Screen Actors Guild (SAG):** SAG has over 120,000 members, but only about 5 percent make their living solely from acting. Membership does require professional experience, however. SAG was formed in the 1930s to combat unfair studio practices and to fight for screen credits, minimum pay rates, benefits, and decent working conditions. The union provides health benefits for members.

Best Practice

Protecting the Environment

The Motion Picture and Television industries have outlined best practices for eliminating waste, reducing their carbon footprint, conserving energy, and promoting recycling. More than half of all studio sets are recycled. In 2008, over 20,000 tons went for recycling rather than conventional waste disposal. It is estimated that this prevented the emission of nearly 34,000 metric tons of greenhouse gasses. New buildings are constructed in accordance with the Leadership in Energy and Environmental Design (LEED) guidelines, which encourage cover water conservation and the use of alternative sources of energy.

→ **Directors Guild of America (DGA):** This union represents over 14,000 members and, according to President Michael Apted, seeks to "protect directorial teams' legal and artistic rights." DGA offers pension and health insurance plans to members.

→ **Writers Guild of America (WGA):** The WGA has over 10,000 members who write for motion pictures, television, and new media. Similar to SAG, WGA functions as a union to offer members financial, legal, and artistic protection. In the early days of motion pictures, up through about the 1950s, studio heads had little appreciation for the talents of writers and treated them poorly, believing they could simply replace one writer with another. Pension and health insurance benefits are available through WGA.

→ **Producers Guild of America (PGA):** This is a professional association for anyone in the producer's unit, from assistant or line producers up through executive producers.

→ **Independent Film Producers (IFP):** This professional association for independent filmmakers has supported the production of 7,000 films and provided resources to over 20,000 independent filmmakers.

➡ **International Alliance of Theatrical and Stage Employees (IATSE):** The IATSE is the umbrella for many local unions, which represent over 115,000 people working in movies, television, and theater. IATSE represents those working in production and postproduction, including multimedia artists, animators, grips, costume designers, makeup and hair artists, and other craftspeople.

➡ **The Teamsters Union:** This union represents the truck drivers who transport goods while a production is on location.

See Chapter 6 for more information about unions and professional associations.

What Is Next?

The film industry is going through an exciting time. It is on the cusp of yet another evolution as it adapts to the growth and refinement of technology, which allows the delivery of Hollywood hits direct to the home. After going through the "scares" of television and home video, the industry is approaching this change much more calmly, realizing it will figure out a way to morph and to make money. This is an exciting time for the independent filmmaker as well. These innovative filmmakers are testing ways to use online technology to publicize their films, to distribute them, and, hopefully, to make money from them. During a period of economic hardship, the film industry maintained its strength, and, in fact, helped many of those hurt by the failure of other industries. This is a good time to be starting out in the film industry.

Chapter 3

On the Job

One of the most exciting things about pursuing a career in film is that you may start out not really knowing where you are going and have a lot of fun figuring out where you want to end up. There are so many variations in this industry, which employs bookkeepers and actors, truckers and directors, writers and carpenters—you get the picture. This chapter will describe the many jobs available and give you a sense of where they fit in the industry. It is organized according to the four phases of filmmaking—development, preproduction, production, and postproduction—followed by two sections on the business end—management and support staff. Several key players are involved in several or all stages of filmmaking:

➡ The *producer* is involved from development through post. Since he or she is one of the main forces during development, the job is listed in that section.

➡ The *director* is also involved in all phases. He or she is usually hired during development and plays a key role in preproduction, production, and post. Since the director's most striking work is directing the production itself, this position is described under production.

➡ The *writer's* main role is in development, but he or she is generally consulted throughout production.

A relatively unique feature of the film business is that most people are hired per job. There are, however, small production companies and educational and industrial film companies that maintain small staffs.

There are jobs in the film industry to suit almost any personality type and skill set. One of the themes that holds true in both the filmmaking and business end is that it is vital to get a foot in the door any way you can. Do not consider anything too menial or below you. Once you are in, this is an industry with many paths to move up. In fact, you may not really know where you want to go until you see some jobs in an area first hand. So if you are currently in an entry level job, take heart and prepare for the best.

Development

This is where it all starts. Development begins when someone— usually a producer or writer—has an idea. It ends when someone— a studio or production company executive—says "green light," or "sorry." Very few of the ideas traveling through the development process actually make it to the big screen. During this process corporate and marketing executives analyze the producer's package and decide whether or not they think it is a money-making idea. Sometimes, the producer involves a writer to create a treatment (idea summary) or even a full script, if the studio asks for it, as part of the package. In some cases, the writer approaches the producer with an idea. Everyone's attorneys and agents are involved as the deal inches toward a reality. From development, you either go on to preproduction or you go home. Most people go home.

Agent

Some agents are former lawyers, some were in the business (actors or writers), and some come straight out of high school or college. Most start out in the mailroom of a talent agency and learn who's who as they sort and deliver mail. The ones who show potential are put through the agency's training program where they work as assistants to agents. Those who are hard working, aggressive, energetic, deal closers become junior agents and then agents. There are several major agencies, such as William Morris Endeavor Entertainment, Creative Artists Agency, and International Creative Management, and there are boutique agencies, with fewer than 20 clients.

Best Practice

Smaller vs. Bigger

Do not use the job descriptions given here to decide what you will not do, what is not your job. Basically, anything your boss asks you to do is your job. If you work on a smaller production you will undoubtedly work in many of these roles at the same time. In other words, the needs are similar regardless of production size—planning, scheduling, shooting, and coordinating—but they can be performed with people doing multiple jobs. On the other hand, if you work on a large production where all these roles are filled, be careful not to step on a colleague's toes unless they give you explicit permission. Your career will benefit in different ways depending on the size of the production. If you are involved in a major production you will see the way the whole thing comes together. You will also see which jobs you may want to aim for in the future. If you are on a smaller production, however, you will get a lot more experience by assuming different roles.

Some agents work independently or with a partner. These people usually have loyal clients when they start their own business. To make a good living the agent has to sell, sell, sell. He or she needs to have a sense of which actor will get which part, which writer will deliver the script that is wanted. The agent gets 10 percent of the client's payment on each project.

The image of the agent is changing. Nowadays few agents have time to really get to know their clients and to help them choose roles or assignments that will further their career. Today's agents primarily want to close a deal. If you want to spend more time with clients, get to know them better, focus on how to guide their career, you might prefer the role of manager.

Associate Producer

Reporting directly to the producer, the associate producer handles various functions delegated by the producer. The associate producer is usually someone who has worked in lower level production jobs.

Attorney

Attorneys who yearn for the glamorous world of the motion picture industry have many different options. Just like any major corporation, every movie studio has an in-house legal department. There are also different law firms that have studios, production companies, writers, actors, producers, and directors as clients. Most creative talent will consult an attorney before signing contracts or negotiating deals. You essentially have the option of practicing corporate law, working for a studio, or working for a law firm with actors, directors, and writers for clients. If you are a litigator you might look for work with the firm that handles lawsuits on behalf of the studio. Different firms handle different types of clients, of course, to avoid conflict of interest. For example, a firm would not represent a studio and actors who may do work for that studio. If you love the movie industry but want the security of a law practice, this can be a perfect situation for you.

Executive Producer

The executive producer supervises one or more producers. This may be a studio executive position to whom the producers of multiple movies report. Although the executive producer must have good instincts in terms of which movies will make it, this is primarily an executive position concerned with finances. Therefore while producers may move in to this position, executive producers can come from other parts of the finance/business side of the business.

Manager

Managers may be former agents or they may have experience in other parts of the business. They must have a solid sense of the business, an ability to guide their client—to tell them what might make the script sell and what look will work at the acting audition, for example. Managers work with only very established clients because they are the only ones who can afford to pay an additional 10 percent (on top of the agent's 10 percent). The manager needs more creative know-how than the agent. For example, a scriptwriter's agent will try to sell the script, but a scriptwriter's manager will first tell the writer how to amend the script to make it more saleable. Managers become intricately involved in their clients' lives. This is not an "early in your career" position. You need a lot of experience in the business and the maturity to engender your client's trust.

Producer

The producer is the CEO of the movie and must have top-notch business, creative, and management skills. The producer's work begins in the development phase and carries through preproduction, production, and postproduction. Producers look for ideas. They read manuscripts, meet with writers, and liaise with agents. During development the producer pulls the package together and shepherds it through the studio executives. To make the package more appealing, the producer often contacts directors and well-known actors during development so that their names can be attached to the project. The producer's package describes the financial as well as the creative elements—why this film is so great, why audiences will love it, and why it will make money. The producer is often involved in obtaining financing for the film, and once production begins the producer is responsible for all financial aspects. From preproduction through production and post, the producer works closely with the director and lead talent to make sure the film stays on schedule and on budget. The director and the line producer report directly to the producer. There are many different "types" of producers and their functions are somewhat different. But when people refer to "the producer"—not line producer, not executive producer, not associate producer—they are talking about the producer described here. To differentiate, see the description of executive producer under management and the description of line producer and assistant producer under production.

Screenwriter

The screenwriter may write a script from scratch—from a personal idea or based on an assignment from a producer—or he or she may develop it from a novel. The first step is to interest a producer with an idea, an idea that the writer pitches verbally or describes briefly in writing. Next the writer submits a treatment. This is a synopsis of the story with a description of what will happen in each scene. The producer and director often ask the writer to make changes they think will make the film better. This can be a collaborative effort with input that makes the script stronger. Or it can be a cause for tension and conflict. If the writer wrote the screenplay from a novel, he or she may also interface with that author—another source of potential conflict.

To become a screenwriter you first must be a good writer, obviously. Many screenwriters work in general editorial jobs for advertising agencies, magazines, or newspapers before undertaking screenwriting. They may then move on to screenwriting jobs for industrial/educational film companies or in house corporate film divisions. The screenwriter needs to come up with a compelling story and present it in a visually interesting manner with realistic dialogue.

Script Consultant

A writer knows that a script submitted to a producer has to be as "perfect" as possible because they may not get another chance. Therefore many well-established screenwriters, and novices also, of course, contract with a script consultant who will offer them feedback and constructive criticism before they turn their script over to the producer. A script consultant provides the type of report ("coverage") your script might get from a script reader—what is right and what is wrong with your script, as well as suggestions for fixing problems. If you want to freelance as a script consultant you must have very strong credentials—credentials that demonstrate your ability to know just what a studio is looking for so that you can guide someone in adjusting their script accordingly. If you are a screenwriter, you want a consultant with solid studio or production company development experience. You then want to see samples of critiques the consultant has done for other writers and references from other writers. Script consultants generally charge $100 to $1,000, usually $300 to $400 per script.

Script Reader

The first stop for a script submitted to a studio or production company is the story department. Here it is assigned to a script reader to evaluate. The script reader prepares a two-page synopsis, called "coverage," which analyzes the script and backs up the recommendation to "consider" or "pass." Most script readers are freelance. This is a great freelance job for an aspiring screenwriter in terms of what you will learn to help your craft. In terms of what you will earn to support yourself, not so great. Although work is generally plentiful for those with proven ability, the pay is pretty bad—$50 to $60 per script. There are a few well-paid opportunities for members of the Story Analysts Union, but there is a waiting list for these jobs.

Writer's Assistant

This job usually entails research, errands, typing notes, copyediting and proofreading scripts, setting meetings, and returning calls. If you are an aspiring screenwriter you will learn from this job and you may find a mentor in your boss.

Preproduction

This is the planning phase during which a shooting schedule is outlined, locations are set, casting is done, costumes are designed, and sets are built. By this time a director has been hired and he or she, in collaboration with the producer, hires everyone who will be involved in the production (with the exception of local talent for extra work or small parts). This is an interesting time creatively as the producer, director, and writer discuss their vision or visions for the film. It is a logistical challenge to work out details in the most cost-effective manner.

A lot of things are happening at the same time. The director hires a production designer to plan sets and locations that will reflect his or her vision for the film. The production designer then hires an art director, a set designer, and a set decorator. The set designer hires a myriad of people who will create sets, such as construction workers, carpenters, electricians, painters, and so on. To complete the look the costume designer, hair stylist, prop master, and makeup artist will also be responsible to the production designer.

Meanwhile, the casting director is at work looking for actors for all the roles. The lead actors have probably been signed on already. If not, the director and producer will decide who they want for the key roles. But the casting agent will schedule auditions so the director can choose talent for the other parts.

The director is clearly involved from the beginning, but since the lion's share of his or her work is during production, the description for director is in the "Production" subsection of this chapter. The line producer and other people in the producer's and director's units are also beginning to work on shooting arrangements. They are also categorized under "Production" to reflect where most of their work is done.

Art Director

The art director designs all the sets and graphics to reflect the production designer's instructions. When there is no production designer, the art director assumes that role. There are more jobs in the art

On the Cutting Edge

CGI

Computer-generated imagery is turning around the way things are done in the special effects end of the business, and not everyone is happy. Prior to CGI, special effects were divided into optical and mechanical effects—*optical* referring to images created with the camera, and *mechanical* referring to images formed by stunt actors, mechanized props, and other things done during the shoot. Now CGI is allowing filmmakers to achieve some of these effects in a safer, and sometimes less costly, environment. Working at a computer with software such as 3ds Max, Blender, LightWave 3D, Maya, and Autodesk Softimage, artists can create many of these dramatic visual effects on the computer. Extras are concerned that CGI may reduce business for them. CGI can make it look like you have a crowd for less than it will cost to hire hundreds of extras. CGI will also replace stunt actors in certain situations. To differentiate it from special effects created optically or mechanically, CGI effects are referred to a visual effects rather than special effects.

department than in any other segment of the industry. There are illustrators, people who specialize in painting backgrounds, people who draw characters for animation. The list is almost endless. If you have a fine arts background and good computer skills, this could be a perfect path for you.

Carpenters

People in the trades, such as carpenters who build the sets or electricians, are hired through contracts arranged between their companies and the studio or production company.

Casting Director

The director usually contacts the agents for the actors he or she wants for the lead roles. Most other roles are filled with the help of a casting director who often works with a casting agency. The casting director breaks down the script according to role and then finds talent, schedules auditions, arranges callbacks, and negotiates contracts. The casting company finds people by going through its roster, contacting agents, or advertising in show business press. You can start in any entry level production job and then look for a junior level job under the casting director.

Construction Coordinator

Taking the plans from the set designers, the construction coordinator manages the crew that builds the sets. This person functions similar to a contractor doing home renovations.

Costume Designer

The costume designer starts with research—what were dresses like in the 1890s? What are they wearing on Wall Street today? The designer then either designs costumes that will be made for the movie or obtains existing costumes from the studio or a rental company. This person also oversees fitting the costumes to each actor. The costume designer reports to the production designer.

Key Costumer

Reporting to the costume designer, the key costumer helps with the selection, acquisition, and maintenance of clothing and accessories. You can begin in production and try to move into this position.

Production Designer

The production designer gets involved early in preproduction to design the entire physical look of the film. The production designer makes sure that all visual elements—sets, graphics, animation, and live footage, for example—convey the feel and the emotion the director wants. The production designer works closely with the producer and director, trying to understand how they see the movie and to create a look that will reflect their vision. The production designer supervises the search for locations and the design of sets. If there is no set designer, he or she also oversees the building and the dressing of all sets. To make sure there is a consistent style, costume designers, hair stylists, make up artists, and set designers are all responsible to the production designer.

Prop Master

Is it raining in that scene? Should the star be carrying an umbrella? Would not people working in an office need computers? If you are filming a baseball game, you better have bats and balls. The prop master breaks down the script and determines what props are needed in each scene. In addition to obtaining the props and maintaining them in good condition, the prop master makes sure the right props are on the set when needed. This is a position that can be reached from a variety of positions in production.

Set Decorator

The set decorator works closely with the production designer and chooses furniture, drapes, and other pieces to decorate sets. Someone doing interior decorating might look toward a job as a set decorator.

Set Designer

The set designer takes the drawings from the art director and turns them in to detailed blueprints. She or he then oversees the construction of all sets. Carpenters, painters, plasterers, landscape artists—anyone involved in set creation reports to the set designer. The set designer reports to the production designer. This is a job that requires specific artistic and architectural skills.

Production

The producer, director, and, to a lesser extent, the writer, are involved in all phases, from development through postproduction. Under the producer and director, two of the key jobs on the set are the line producer and the assistant director. The line producer will be one of the first people hired by the director and producer. Although the line producer reports to the producer, he or she works for the director as well. Together the line producer and the first assistant director (AD) keep everything going during filming. They coordinate call times for crew and actors and maintain the budget. Under the line producer, the producer's unit includes a unit production manager, production coordinators and assistants (better known as PAs), and an accountant. The director's unit includes a first assistant director, a second unit director, a director of photography, and the production designer.

The production designer, described under preproduction, and the director of photography (DOP) are two of the top people helping the director achieve his or her vision. The production designer creates the physical sets to be photographed and the director of photography figures out how to photograph them. Sometimes conflicts arise between these two top people. The DOP may feel that the production designer created a set that is "impossible to film." ("Where can I put the lights?!") The camera and lighting teams work together to create the images wanted by the DOP. The sound engineer and microphone operators are responsible for making sure there is clear, high-quality sound in every scene.

While actors are being filmed on the set, animators and artists are off in another studio preparing graphics and special effects. The art department is generally the largest department on a movie. Job growth for talented artists with excellent computer skills is about the best in the industry.

Actors

Actors are categorized into those who are part of the cast and have lines and those who are "background," the extras. Extras are the unidentified people in crowd scenes (at parties, in subway stations, at concerts, or in offices, for example). People that do stunt work, narration, voiceover, and cameos are also considered actors. Most actors have had some formal training, whether it was in the drama program at a university, at a theater-sponsored program, or in an independent dramatic arts school.

Actors may respond to calls for auditions advertised in newspapers, such as *Variety, Drama-Logue, Casting Call,* and *Backstage,* or their agent may tell them about a call. The producer and director scan the photographs to find "the look" they want, and then call those people in for auditions. It is important for actors to realize that the director has an image of what he or she wants for each character. Rejections usually are based on not being the type wanted for that role rather than a referendum on acting ability. Even when an actor passes the photo test, delivery or style during the audition may differ from what the director envisioned.

Once an actor has a few credits, he or she may be able to get an agent, and the agent will arrange auditions for them. You have to be generating a fair amount of income or be seen as having a lot of potential for an agent to work with you.

Animator/Visual Effects Artists

Also called multimedia artists, animators and visual effects artists use illustrations and computers to create moving characters and special effects. If the entire movie will be in animation or if animation plays an important role, the animator may be consulted in the development phase. The bulk of the animator's work, however, is during the production phase.

Assistant Camera Operator

Depending on the size of the production there may be one, two, or three camera assistants. When there are three, the first assistant handles focus and exposure; the second assistant backs up the first and runs to get lenses, film, whatever is needed; and the third is responsible for the film and spends much of the time in the darkroom. There is a complete team (camera operator and assistants) for each camera on the set. They are identified by letter—Camera A, B, and so on. Most camera operators have a college degree; many majored in film. The path here would be from third assistant, to second assistant, to first assistant, to camera operator. Many camera operators aspire to become a director of photography or cinematographer.

Assistant Director

Depending on the size of the production, there may be first and second assistants who report to the director and help with noncreative details, such as handling the transportation of equipment, making sure talent is ready and a scene is set before the crew is ready to shoot, hiring extras, caterers, and so forth. In essence, the assistant director makes sure everything and everyone is ready before the director and stars are there to shoot a particular scene. The first AD works closely with the line producer to establish call times for crew and talent and to make sure the production schedule is followed. On a large production there may be a second assistant director who reports to the first AD. Usually this person prepares and distributes daily paperwork, call sheets, production reports, and SAG contracts and makes sure the cast and crew are in the right place at the right time. On a really big production, there is a second second AD who helps the first AD and is usually in charge of extras.

Best Boy Grip

As assistant to the key grip, the best boy grip takes care of the equipment and recruits additional crew manpower when needed. There are a lot of families where one generation after another becomes a grip or a gaffer.

Boom Operator

The boom operator works for the sound engineer and handles the boom mic during the filming, moving it from person to person. The boom mic is a fairly large microphone on the end of a long pole.

Camera Operator

The camera operator maneuvers the camera, frames the shot, and shoots. He or she works closely with the gaffer since the shot must be properly lit. On a smaller production, the camera operator and cinematographer are one in the same. But on a larger production the camera operator follows the guidance of the cinematographer, or director of photography.

Director

Everyone wants to be a director. Even famous actors yearn for a chance to direct a movie. It is an understandable goal because the director is truly the person whose vision is reflected in the film. The director is the one in charge during production, but he or she is really involved in all phases of filmmaking. He or she is often solicited by the producer during development to take part in elucidating the vision of the film. During preproduction, the director auditions talent and makes casting decisions and directs rehearsals.

The director has the final say on location choice, casting, set design, costumes, music, and everything that will impact the look and feel of the production. But it is in the production phase that the director is star and the success or failure of the film rests on his or her shoulders. It is the director's vision that brings the script to life and turns it into a compelling movie. It is the director's talent and managerial skill that turns the actors into the characters they play. It is the director's eye that oversees the creation of sets that convince the viewer that this is World War II, the Victorian era, or the future. The director oversees camera angles, lighting, and sound. The director's work is creative but he or she works closely with the producer to make sure the movie stays on schedule and on budget. The director may be in charge but he or she may have to cajole an irritated actor in order to keep the show moving. The director also works with the editor in postproduction to make sure his or her vision is maintained as scenes are chosen. A good director knows every aspect of filming from working the camera, to acting, to writing.

Most independent filmmakers learn directing on-the-job by directing their own films. Some people move up from the assistant director spot. There is an assistant director course offered jointly by the Directors Guild of America and the Alliance of Motion Picture and Television Producers. Working for a company that produces industrial films or a small theatrical production company may help you acquire the skills you need to be hired as an assistant director.

Director of Photography (Cinematographer)

The DOP works closely with the director and figures out how to photograph in a way that reflects the director's vision. This means orchestrating camera framing, lighting, and so forth. The DOP heads the camera and lighting teams, which include the gaffer, key grip, etc. Experience in lighting or camera or, preferably, both is a good background for this job. Like the producer and director positions, however, there has to be a certain natural talent, a good eye, underneath the experience in order to succeed in this role. If you are just starting out, working as an assistant camera person and then as a camera operator may put you in a good jumping-off position for this job. Alternatively, some film school graduates obtain this position based on the success of their independent film school productions.

Keeping
in Touch

Make Waiting Work for You

"It's who you know," is a phrase that may be applied to getting a job by someone whose uncle is, say, a producer. But people without relatives or friends in the field can forge relationships that will guide them through the early years of their career. Although shooting involves long hours and hard work, it also involves a lot of sitting around. There is waiting for the scene to be lit, waiting for a set to be broken down, waiting for the actor to change clothes, waiting, waiting, and waiting. What you do with the waiting can greatly impact your career. Talk to people whose work interests you. Show interest; ask questions. Offer to help. Helping a senior person, making his or her job easier, is a great way to find a mentor. Do not shy away from menial work. Getting coffee got a bad name when it was a task female secretaries did for their male bosses. But regardless of your gender, or that of your superior, getting coffee is a nice thing to do. People want to help people who are nice to them, who make things better for them. Make sure that you are seen as someone with initiative, not a pain in the neck. Remember that everyone is there to work. You are not being paid to learn and your potential mentors are not being paid to teach you. That said, many pros thrive on the opportunity to teach, to guide and to help someone into the next step of their career. Your mentors can teach you the tricks of the trade, the way to do things faster, easier, better. They can also tell you who is looking for someone with your talents, introduce you, and put in a good work for you. This is a much more effective way of moving up in the business than reading ads. A good word from a trusted pro is the best way to move into a better position.

Dolly Grip

This is a great job if you wish you could fly. Dollies are the platforms on which you put a camera when you want to shoot from above. The dolly has a hydraulic arm that lowers and raises the platform. The dolly grip maintains the dollies and makes sure they are where they are needed.

Gaffer

The gaffer is responsible to the DOP for all lighting set ups and procedures. The gaffer selects the type of lights for a scene and decides where to place them. The gaffer also works closely with the key grip. A reasonable career path might be from best boy grip to grip to gaffer. Similar to grip jobs, there are many "gaffer families."

Grip

The crew member responsible for set up, adjustment, and maintenance of production equipment. The grip may assist with camera movement, lighting, and rigging.

Hair Stylist

The hair stylist works with the make-up artist and costume designer to create a unified look. In addition to setting the schedule for each actor, the hair stylist cuts, colors, and styles both wigs and natural hair. The hair stylist coordinates with the production designer.

Key Grip

The key grip is responsible to the DOP and the gaffer for providing and placing all diffusion and for moving, setting up, striking, and transporting lights. Moving into a gaffer position would be a good move up from here.

Line Producer

The line producer is usually hired by the producer and director early in the production phase. Although the line producer reports directly to the producer, he or she will usually work for the director as well. During the production phase the line producer figures the budget for any given day and organizes the process of production in the most cost effective way. For example, he or she will try to clump scenes for each actor together in order to limit the number of days any actor must work and be paid. The line producer works closely with the first assistant director and is assisted by the production accountant, production assistants, production coordinator, and unit production manager.

Make-up

The make-up artist works with the hair stylist and costume designer to coordinate the look for each character, sets schedules for makeup application, oversees application, and recruits and oversees make-up artists who specialize in body makeup and special effects. In a sizeable production there will be assistant makeup artists as well.

Production Assistant

Also known as a PA, this is a typical entry level position for those interested in any job in filmmaking. The role varies from set to set. For a feature film this position usually includes running errands, getting catering, calling truckers, and similar tasks. Sometimes a production assistant is assigned to a major director or actor as a one-on-one assistant during a production. For a small, low budget production the PA position may encompass some of the work allocated to the assistant directors on a higher budget film. You will see everything and learn a lot if you land a job as a production assistant. You will begin to get a sense of where you would like to move up. Are you very interested in camera or lighting? Sound? Directing or producing? Writing? Obviously there are many steps between PA and any of these positions, but at least you will have a better idea of where you want to travel once you have some experience on the set. A PA can start up the path to producer by doing a fantastic job, a job in which the producer sees how much help the PA has been. That can move you up to assistant producer pretty quickly.

Production Coordinator

Reporting to the line producer, this position coordinates logistics, ships film, gets dailies, arranges transportation and accommodations, and deals with any emergencies that arise. The production coordinator usually sets up production and writing offices on location and liaises between the production office and the set. This is a high pressure, detail oriented job that requires good follow up skills. It will put you in a good place for a job further up the producer's ladder.

Production Manager

A production manager oversees the unit production managers. When a film is being shot in more than one location simultaneously, there will be a unit production manager at each location.

Script Supervisor

The script supervisor follows the shooting script as each scene is shot. He or she records information vital to the director and editor next to each take. For instance, was the shot a close up or a wide shot? This way if the editor wants to cut from a wide shot to a close up of the lead character he or she knows where to find each shot. What was the actress wearing? Making notes about clothing, hair, and accessories is important for continuity. Does the actor walk through the door and come out on the other side in a different outfit? Unless the actor is playing Superman, this is not supposed to happen. But when you shoot a script out of sequence it can easily happen if someone is not checking. The script supervisor also notes any problems with the take or anything special about the take. Did the actor flub his lines? Then the editor does not have to review that take.

Sound Mixer

The production sound mixer or "sound man," is responsible to the director for the quality of sound recorded for each scene. Like most crew positions, the sound mixer is hired on a freelance basis for a particular production. The sound mixer meets with the producer and director prior to production to discuss their creative goals, technical needs, and budget. The mixer also connects with the costume department and camera crew to find out about anything that will restrict the use of certain microphones. In addition, he or she surveys different locations to be prepared for potential problems. This person selects microphones, adjusts the levels of mixers and synthesizers during the shoot, and supervises boom operators and sound assistants. He or she makes sure that the background noise is the same for scenes that will appear close together and they record adequate room tone, or ambient sound, for the editor to use in post. Right before you strike the set in a location, you will hear the sound mixer yell, "Quiet. Room tone." Room tone can be used in post to make dialogue recorded in two different locations sound the same. Sound mixers also record or oversee recording of all sound on the set. Advancement is generally from sound trainee to sound assistant, to boom operator, to sound mixer. If you are seriously interested in sound and you have trouble landing a trainee position, you might first try to learn about the equipment by getting a job at an equipment manufacturer. Anyone working on the sound crew must have a very good ear and must be "grounded" in electronics. It may be that people who work in sound are born, not made. Most people in production and postproduction sound will tell you about their childhood love of sound manipulation. People often begin in postproduction sound, move up through the ranks, and then move into production sound, which pays better and is considered more exciting to some.

Sound Recordists

Sound recordists set up and run the individual tape recorders. Computer courses in digital sound and electronic mixing can help a boom operator move into the sound mixer position.

Stunt Person

The people who do stunts are considered actors and may join the Screen Actors Guild. If you almost made the Olympic gymnast team or if your parents called you "monkey" because you were always swinging from trees, you might enjoy this work. You need to be a bit of a thrill seeker but you also need training to be able to perform stunts safely.

Unit Production Manager

Reporting to the line producer, this position protects the producer's financial interests by monitoring the budget and schedule and trying to get the most cost-effective deals with companies or freelancers helping with the production. The unit production manager works closely with the production accountant, tracks expenditures, and pays bills.

Postproduction

By the time production is over it is difficult to imagine what the finished movie will be like. Scenes have been shot out of order, so no one has followed the storyline chronologically for a while. Scenes have been shot many times and from many different angles. Some scenes may have been filmed simultaneously in different locations. While filming was going on, artists and animators were at work preparing titles, graphics, and artwork. A musical score was composed. In postproduction all the footage, all the art, and all the graphics come together under the sure hands of an editor. New York-based screenwriter and actor, Bill Wilson, describes the editor as doing "the final rewrite of the script."

While the editor is working his or her magic, the sound team is fixing anything that was not recorded clearly and adding special effects and music. Like the sound team in production, most members of the sound team in post have been fascinated with sound since childhood. Most begin work as runners (doing errands and menial tasks) in a postproduction sound facility. They then move up through the sound positions outlined here. They do not move up quickly. It takes a lot of experience in each position to be ready for the next. There are courses and training programs described in Chapter 6, which you may want to take before or while you are working in an entry level position.

The structure of post is as follows: The postproduction supervisor keeps both the editor and the sound team on schedule and on budget. Across from the editor, the sound team is led by a sound supervisor who is often also the sound designer. Under them, you will find the audio recording engineer, and then the ADR, Foley, and music editors and their assistants.

Audio Recording Engineers

Audio recording engineers, or sound effects editors, manipulate different parts of the sound track—the dialogue, music, and background sound—to fit the picture. Like much of the other postproduction work, this function is becoming increasingly computer driven. If you are interested in sound, be it on the set or in post, you might try to get a job at a radio station or doing music videos before moving into the film area. Or, if you have a job as a PA or another entry level position, speak to the sound engineers on the set.

Automated Dialogue Replacement Editor

Also known as ADR dialogue editor or ADR mixer, this is the person who makes sure the best audio is used for each scene. Since the same dialogue is recorded numerous times through different takes and with different camera angles, the ADR has a lot from which to choose. When all this fails, however, the ADR has to work with the actor to re-record the problematic lines. This can be tricky because it can be difficult for the actor to deliver the lines in question exactly the way he did when the film was shot. The ADR has to function as director, gauging the actor's performance and doing repeat takes if necessary. To avoid holding up post because an actor is not in town, ADR sessions can take place with the actor in one location and the ADR in another location with the use of an integrated services digital network (ISDN). The ISDN transmits the audio using end-to-end digital connectivity. The ADR Mixer reports to the sound supervisor and coordinates with other members of the sound postproduction team. Like other senior jobs in postproduction sound, it takes years of experience working through all the junior positions to become an ADR.

Composer

The producer and director may contract a composer to write an original score for the movie.

Editor

The creativity of the editor and his or her ability to reflect the director's vision is essential to the impact of the final product. An editor can make or break a film, and many directors will work only with certain editors, some with only one particular editor. The editor carefully selects best takes and cuts them together to tell the story in the most interesting, emotive, and visually appealing manner. Whether the editor chooses to insert a close-up of a listener's tears, or uses a slow dissolve rather than a cut, has a tremendous impact on the feel of the film. Today, almost all editing is done digitally. Many editors began as camera operators or as editing room assistants.

Editor's Assistant

There are many jobs for assistant editors, who usually organize footage for editors, making sure every shot is accounted for, and handle all technical issues so that the editor can apply creativity to the process. This is a great entry level job because you will learn a lot about cinematography and editing. Aspiring writers will also learn ways to improve their scripts by working for an editor.

Foley Editor

Named after Jack Foley from Universal Studios, Foley editors add the subtle sounds that microphones often miss during production—the rustling of clothes, soft footsteps, etc. He or she also enhances major sound effects like explosions or car crashes. There are Foley mixers and Foley artists working for the Foley editor to create or obtain these sounds. The Foley editor reports to the sound supervisor and liaises with other members of the post sound team. He or she usually starts at the bottom and works up through the sound hierarchy.

Music Editor

The music editor liaises between the composer and the director to ensure that music is used to accentuate and complement the live action, not overpower it. He or she takes part in the "spotting session" with the director and other members of postproduction sound to ensure a coordinated effect. The music editor may create the music sound track from a number of different sources, including a score composed for the movie and the purchase of other music. The music editor uses a special computer software program to lay down the music tracks in sync with the picture. A detailed "cue sheet" (a breakdown of the music used) is sent to the American Society of Composers, Authors, and Publishers so that royalties will be paid any time the film is screened. Many music editors are talented musicians who work their way up through the other jobs in the sound department. The music editor reports to the supervising sound editor and liaises with the other sound editors.

Postproduction Supervisor

The postproduction supervisor coordinates all visual and audio facets of the edit and is responsible for making sure it runs as smoothly and as cost effectively as possible. Although everyone hears about the months a movie can spend filming on location, few people realize that the postproduction period often takes longer than production and is a very expensive process. The job of postproduction supervisor requires an understanding of all jobs in post and excellent organizational skills.

Sound Designer

On many productions, one person functions as both sound designer (also known as sound effects editor or special effects editor) and supervising sound editor. The sound designer is responsible for identifying where special sound effects are needed—such as a gunshot, dog barking, or door closing—and producing those effects. Sometimes the designer can use an existing effect; other times he or she has to create the effect. If you are wondering whether or not this is a creative job, consider the sound designer who imagined and then created a dinosaur roar from a slowed down voice that was reversed, pitched up, and reverberated. This job obviously requires a naturally good ear, creativity, and many years of training. Most people who become sound designers can remember being fascinated by sound manipulation as kids. Sound designers usually start out as runners in postproduction houses, work their way up to becoming sound assistants, and then go on to higher positions. The sound designer reports to the sound supervisor, if they are not one in the same, and works in tandem with other members of the sound editing team. Sound designers also need to be good with computers since they must lay all sound effects on a digital audio workstation (DAW).

Supervising Sound Editor

The supervising sound editor is responsible for making sure the director's vision is reflected in the final product. After the filming is over, the supervising sound editor and other sound editors attend a "spotting session" with the director in which they discuss concepts for the overall feel of sound in the film. This is a managerial position, and the supervising sound editor must make sure that all facets of sound postproduction are on schedule and on budget. The supervising sound editor will also liaise with the postproduction supervisor. This position is usually filled by the same person who is doing sound design, or special effects editing, for the film. This is the highest position in the sound post department and requires many years of experience and exceptional skill. Most supervising sound editors began at the bottom and have worked through every other job in sound postproduction.

Studio Management

The management team at a studio is like the management team at any major corporation—it strives to create a product that will sell in the marketplace. It develops an efficient organization system so that costs are minimized and profits are maximized. Management includes marketing, business, and financial professionals. The thing that is different at a motion picture studio is that many think it is glamorous and everyone knows it is stressful. The stakes are high. If you give the green light to a movie that flops, people may not remember the two blockbusters you brought in last year. "Three strikes and you are out," is the motto. But people do not need three strikes to get fired. People come and go often based on what seem to be the slightest misunderstandings.

In some industries, it is difficult to move up from a junior position, to break free of the "kid" image. Not so in entertainment. Get your foot in the door, demonstrate your smarts, and you are on your way, says David Rensin in *The Mailroom: Hollywood History from the Bottom Up*. That is why some Harvard MBAs are willing to start out in the mailroom job, according to Rensin. This is a field where super smart, young, energetic, and aggressive people with great ideas can work hard, get noticed, and get ahead. The descriptions of positions in this section relate to the motion picture studio. You will also find executive and management teams at production houses, postproduction houses, talent agencies, and public relations firms.

In most corporations, the organizational chart begins with the chief executive officer (CEO), who reports to the board. A variety of vice presidents in charge of different areas of the corporation (usually finance, marketing, and business) report to the CEO. Under the VPs are middle managers and under them, support staff. Each company will be a little different, however. Job titles vary from company to company and there are several levels in each group. For example, there may be assistants, associates, junior managers, managers, directors, and vice presidents in marketing. Unless you are moving from one studio to another and have already achieved some level of success, you will probably start in an assistant position and work your way up. There are two middle management jobs discussed here that you will not find in every type of business—creative executives and development executives.

Accountants

Most accountants are college graduates with a CPA. There are management accounting jobs in the studios, in large production companies, and in post houses. There are also accounting firms that consult with and audit the studios. If you want to be where the action is, a production accountant is often on the set and works closely with the unit production manager to keep track of finances during filming.

Advertising Manager

The advertising manager is part of the marketing manager's team and focuses on developing an advertising campaign that reflects the themes agreed upon for marketing the movie. The advertising manager has a staff to develop the ads, and other people who report to him or her place the ads on television or in print. Many advertising managers majored in advertising or public relations in college.

Business Manager

An MBA is a helpful degree for a business manager, although someone with business skills may move into this position from accounting or marketing. The business manager is concerned with the efficiency of the organization, with setting up systems to minimize errors, enhance productivity, and maximize profits.

Chief Executive Officer

In a major studio or a sizeable production company there is a CEO who runs everything and reports to a board of directors. All of the top managers listed in this section—the people in charge of distribution, marketing, and financial, for example—report to the CEO. In a smaller company, the CEO is often an owner-producer who personally performs all of these management jobs. Starting out in an assistant position at one of these companies is a great way to learn the business and can help you land a job at a major studio. The CEO may be an expert in the film industry who also has business skills, or may be an MBA with strong business skills who is learning the film industry.

Development Executives and Creative Executives

Better known as DEs and CEs, the studio gatekeepers are just below the vice president level and way above the assistant level. In *Breakfast with Sharks*, Michael Lent describes DEs and CEs as having "rapid fire intelligence." He goes on to write, "These people are in their twenties and their thirties and work frenetically cruel schedules six and seven days a week." They are aggressive and ambitious, eager to bring in the next blockbuster. But they are terrified of sponsoring a flop. Getting fired after a short spin is not uncommon.

Distribution Manager

In the film business, the distribution manager and marketing manager's work is intertwined. The distributor tries to identify a target audience during the development phase, because without a good shot at a good audience no one would give a green light to the project. In addition to being knowledgeable about marketing and promotion, the distribution manager needs specific knowledge about distribution outlets and trends. Should this film be released in the summer or winter? Should it open in a few theaters and then spread out or should it hit many theaters simultaneously? When should it be available for DVD? For pay TV? For cable? What about online? The distribution manager has to consider all this with a view toward maximizing profits from each outlet before moving on to the next. A successful distribution manager needs to be a good marketer with a strategic knowledge of distribution. Working in an assistant position for a distributor or for someone in marketing, advertising, or promotion will put you in the right position to move into this end of the business.

Marketing Manager

The marketing manager may be consulted during the development process when studio executives and the producer are debating whether or not to produce a particular film. The marketing manager is thinking, "Can I make a go of this; can I lure people to the theater? Who is the audience for this?" By the time production begins the marketing manager has developed a strategy. While the director, crew, and talent are filming, the marketing manager is back at the studio figuring out how to promote what they film. Advertising and promotion managers report to the marketing manager and together they outline the strategy and schedule. They work closely with the distribution manager. What will the focus be? How will they "brand" this film? What will be the central theme of all their promotion? With their staffs, they produce trailers to precede movies currently in theaters, prepare advertisements for television and print media, and write press releases. Have you ever noticed how common it is for a guest on one of the television talk shows to have a book or a movie about to be released? The promotion staff sets up these appearances as well as magazine interviews.

Promotion Manager

Part of the marketing manager's team, the promotion manager writes the press releases and biographies of lead actors, which will be used to generate appearances for and articles about the actors. The publicist also contacts television and radio hosts to try to get a spot for one of the lead actors on the show. The publicist maintains relationships with news and magazine editors and tries to interest them in doing an interview with one of the stars. Promotion managers often major in marketing, public relations, advertising, journalism, or English in college. It helps to have a first job on the "other side"—writing for a magazine or assisting on production of a TV show. The important thing is having contacts that may be more likely to interview your client because of their relationship with you. Some people, however, can start in a very junior position in a promotion department and make contacts and work their way up, from errand runner and coffee getter to unit publicist.

Unit Publicist

If you are interested in promotion but yearn to be on the set, traveling from location to location, becoming a unit publicist may be just the right mix for you. The unit publicist travels with the crew. In addition to getting ideas by watching the production, the unit publicist tries to generate publicity wherever the crew is filming. He or she tries to get actors on local radio and television shows. The publicist invites journalists to visit the set and write stories.

Sales Agent

What about the independent films? The films with no studio or staff behind them? The sole filmmaker seeking a distributor? Enter the sales agent to represent the filmmaker and help him or her find a distributor. Sales agents go to festivals looking for new talent. Like any agent, the film sales agent needs an eye for talent and for what will sell. Structuring the deal is also a vital part of this job. The sales agent needs a strong business background—preferably an MBA—marketing skills, and a ton of charm. Once a deal is made, the sales agent pays the filmmaker a percentage of profits.

Support Staff

"Get any job you can," advises screenwriter and actor Bill Wilson. "The important thing is to just get on the lot, even if it is just to drive a truck through," he adds. Some of the support jobs are pretty interesting and offer the opportunity to make great contacts and learn the business.

Assistants

Assistants work like crazy and often take a lot of abuse from their bosses—but this is a great job for early in your career. It is a perfect "stepping stone" job. Producers, executives, agents, managers, and some directors and writers have assistants. At large companies—studios, large agencies, or production companies—assistants are often rotated from one executive to the next until the right fit is found. Meanwhile, the assistant is learning a different aspect of the business and making new contacts each time. Assistants handle whatever their bosses throw at them (unfortunately, sometimes literally) from typing letters, reading scripts, picking out gifts, to picking up the dry cleaning. The biggest function in most assistant positions is handling the phone. Your boss will get hundreds of calls a day, many of them from people you cannot irritate, such as leading actors, star directors, and potential investors. Some of these people are short tempered and have big egos. You will have to figure out a way to make them feel special even if you have had to put them on hold. As you work as an assistant, you will probably get a feel for where you want to go in the industry. Do you like being headquartered at the studio and dealing with marketing or promotion? Or do you covet the excitement of location shooting?

Bookkeepers

Bookkeepers are needed in all business offices, and this is a great way to make you invaluable and to find a mentor. You'll even see bookkeepers in the credits of some movies. Some bookkeepers learn the skill at a junior college, but others teach themselves with Quick-Books, a popular software program. You might want to pursue your degree part time while working as a bookkeeper and become an accountant. There are jobs for accountants in the office and on the set.

Mailroom Clerk

You think it is only in the movies that mailroom clerks end up as movie moguls? In his fascinating book, *The Mailroom: Hollywood History from the Bottom Up*, David Rensin reveals that some of today's leaders in the entertainment industry—including Barry Diller, Michael Ovitz, and David Geffen—started out in the mailroom of an agency. Sorting and delivering mail can be the first step en route to a job as an agent—from mail clerk, to trainee, to assistant, to junior agent, to—the sky's the limit.

Trade Jobs

These include jobs support jobs in fields such as catering and transportation. People "in the business" usually advise those starting out to do anything they have to, to get on the set. Once you are there you can begin to learn the business and make contacts. Jobs in transportation and catering can be a lead in, although many transportation jobs come under the auspices of the Teamsters Union.

Chapter 4

Tips for Success

It is who you know. But it is not WHO you know. People have always tried to discourage other people's interest in a career in film by warning them that it is almost impossible to break in unless you know someone. These people—parents, relatives, well-meaning friends—are talking about someone "big," like the guy who helped Tori Spelling get started, or Sofia Coppola's dad.

In truth, most people with successful careers in the industry do not have the ear of a famous director, actor, or producer. They have, however, made meaningful contacts early in their careers, and these contacts have helped them. When the senior people they work with on one job are hired for another production, they recommend them to the director or producer. The producer wants to hire a known quantity and feels a lot more comfortable with someone recommended by a pro than with someone who responds to an ad. When a movie is a success, producers often like to keep the "good luck" team together for the next show. Next to talent, ability, and a good work ethic, the ability to network and find a mentor are the most crucial keys to success in the film business. You must be able to get along with others, to convince them of your talent and ability, and to make them like you and want to help you.

This first section of this chapter discusses effective networking in the film industry. It is geared to anyone near the beginning of their career in any aspect of film, from the studio set to the boardroom. Subsequent sections in this chapter discuss how you can move up the ladder in different occupations.

Luck Matters

A unique aspect of the film business is that most people are not full-time salaried employees. Many people who work in filmmaking—producers, directors, writers, actors, cinematographers, and crew members, for example—are usually hired on a project-by-project basis. When a shoot goes well people often feel their colleagues are good luck. When they get their next job, they will recommend you to the director. Even people in staff positions, such as those in studio management, move around a lot. Assistants on their way up may be rotated from one executive to another in rapid sequence. Sometimes it is because the studio is training them. Sometimes it is just because a need arose. Very smart middle management people are often fired at the drop of a hat. Something did not work out. They saw a project differently from the way their boss saw it.

Keeping in Touch

E-Mail

When you meet an industry professional at a seminar or screening or on the set, remember to send an e-mail the next day, while the person still remembers you. Make it an informal, friendly note. Let them know you enjoyed meeting them. Maybe comment on something that happened at the event or add a few thoughts about a conversation you had. Do not ask for a job. Do not ask for anything. Just engage the person as a "business friend." Keep in touch. Share information to help them when you can. The more you help others, the more they will want to help you.

Off the Set: Places to Meet People

Getting to know people and finding a mentor are the most important ways to get ahead in any aspect of the film business. Well, what if you are not working right now? What if you have a job but you are not making many contacts? What if you just want to make more contacts? Good idea. You need to be meeting as many people as possible.

Some people find a solid core group in film school. If you went to film school, consider arranging a get together for some of your buds. If you are going to film school while you work, be helpful to your peers at school. Offer to help them on their films. The more you do of your work, the more you work on other people's shows, the more you have to put on a reel to show potential employers.

The Producer's Guild of America (PGA), the Directors Guild of America (DGA), the Writers Guild of America (WGA), and the American Film Institute (AFI) host seminars and events in New York and Los Angeles and through local chapters in other parts of the country. You will learn from the seminars, of course, and you will also have the opportunity to connect with producers, directors, writers, studio reps, and agents. In his book, *Breakfast with Sharks*, screenwriter Michael Lent suggests that rather than just attending a seminar, you should volunteer to help. Lent writes about volunteering at the Key West Film and Literature Symposium, where he was asked to help one of the panelists who was a speaker later that day. The panelist was William Goldman, author of *Butch Cassidy and the Sundance Kid*. Lent says, "The time spent with him changed my life." You can also find courses and workshops to help you develop your skills and meet other students with whom you can collaborate. Resources are listed in Chapter 6. If you have already relocated to Hollywood or New York, attend screenings and premieres at least once a month. You have a decent chance of making industry contacts at the screenings and you will keep up with what is out there.

When you meet people at industry functions make sure to exchange e-mail addresses. Try to develop an e-mail rapport, chatting about news in the industry and sharing anything that might be of interest to them. Do not ask for a job or a recommendation. Once you have developed a rapport let them know the type of work in which you would be interested. It is also a good idea to join film-related chat rooms on the Internet.

How to Get Your Foot in the Door

It is difficult to get established quickly in the world of film. The industry rewards those who are patient, have a solid work ethic, and who are willing to build a career from the ground up.

Mailroom to Mogul

If you are still near the beginning of your career, it may not be too late to get a job in the mailroom. No, you did not misread that sentence. Outside of Hollywood, people think working your way up from the mailroom is a myth. Maybe one or two moguls did it in the old days when even studio heads did not have college degrees, but no one does it today, do they?

They do. And they have college degrees. Some have MBAs, CPAs, or LLDs. In *The Mailroom: Hollywood History from the Bottom Up*, David Rensin reports that it is easier to get in to Harvard (your chances are one in nine) than in to the mailroom of a major Hollywood talent agency (one in 30). The mailroom is the greatest equalizer in Hollywood. The kid from Iowa has as much chance of getting a job in the agency mailroom as a Hollywood mogul's kid, according to Rensin. Lucky showbiz kids get to work in the mailroom on their summer breaks. But if they want a full-time mailroom job, they have to apply in the fall like everyone else. You must have a college degree, take a basic skills test, and be interviewed by three to ten people. The mailroom is the official first stop in an in-house training program to be a Hollywood agent. But it can get you on the path to any job in the business—marketing, public relations, development or creative executive, producer, director, or writer. This is not work for the faint hearted, and those without the requisite aggression and ambition are usually weeded out during the interview process. The hours are long and the pay is lousy. You work in cramped quarters. People scream at you and ask you to do the impossible. The emblem of the person destined to make it out of the mailroom says "I can take care of it," and then takes care of it.

While slaving away in the mailroom you get two types of training: You see the agents at work and by osmosis get a feel for what you have to do, and you are put through a structured training program with seminars, luncheons, and even tests. You learn all aspects of the business at an agency. You see what is going on at every studio, and this experience can be a useful in teaching you about yourself, about your own temperament.

Temp Agencies to Top Jobs

If you are one of the 29 out of 30 who do not make it into the mailroom training program, or if you do not like mailrooms or do not want to work at a talent agency, consider the tried-and-true world of temping. You will probably earn better money than you will at your chosen craft initially, and it is easier to deal with the frustrations of job hunting and rejections if you are not worried about paying the

INTERVIEW

Prinzi's Principles and Tips for Success

Frank Prinzi, ASC
Emmy Award–winning cinematographer

When did you know you wanted to work in film?
I loved film from the time I was a kid. I was making films with my Super 8 when I was 15. But my parents talked me out of it. I tried to listen to them. I majored in psychology in college. But I just could not stop thinking about it, and I took a few film courses. Eventually I realized I would not be happy in anything else, and I enrolled in the graduate film program at New York University.

Did you find that film school helped your career?
One of the best things about film school was the contacts I made with other aspiring filmmakers. When I graduated I started a film coop with a few fellow graduates and within a short time the group grew to 45 people. We got together once a month to talk about the business, new technology, who was hiring. We also watched and critiqued each other's films.

I understand you do not subscribe to the belief that you have to be cutthroat in a cutthroat business.
Quite the opposite. There are so many sensitive, high-strung, "difficult" people in the film business, people gravitate toward someone who is nice.

That is the first of your 10 tips for making contacts and finding a mentor, is not it? What are the tips you give to young people on the set?
1. Be nice. People have to like you and feel comfortable with you. Whether you are on the set, in a postproduction house, or in the management headquarters of the studio, you will work long hours. That is the nature of film. That means you spend a lot of time with your colleagues. I am sure I've spent more time with my crew than with my wife over the past 10 years.
2. Keep your eye on the ball. You may start out in different jobs while you figure out what you like and do not like, what you are good at and what you are not so great at. You may take dif-

ferent jobs to earn a living. But keep your career goal in mind and look for jobs that will give you the experience you need.

3. Say "yes." Film is a problem-solving business. You have problems to solve from the moment you get on the set. For instance, the other day we were about to shoot an interior scene in which the sun would be streaming through the window. But we were way behind schedule and by the time we got to that room, it was dark outside. The director asked if I could make it look like daylight. He was tired and aggravated that we were behind schedule, and he didn't want to hear "no." I offered him a solution: I would put diffusers over the windows and use lights to make the windows look hot. But I made sure he understood that it would be a very interior look. I made sure he knew what he was getting so he could decide whether that would work for him. Think of a solution. Try to help. Maybe you can't do exactly what the producer or director wants, but what can you do? Instead of "can't be done," how about "if we tweak the...." People are used to hearing complaints, negativity, and a million reasons why someone can't or won't do something. Put yourself in the producer's, director's, or studio executive's shoes. He or she has to get it done, no matter what. So be an ally. Make it easier, not harder.

4. Emanate enthusiasm. Often you genuinely like the film on which you are working. But you are so tired. Everyone is exhausted after four 7 A.M. to 10 P.M. days in a row. Sleep deprivation makes everyone irritable. When you are feeling like that, it is difficult to show enthusiasm even for a film you like. But try. It will be worth it.

5. Be interesting. You are your colleague's social life and (dysfunctional) family. You are together 17 hours a day on the set. In the studio office, they're pulling hours almost that long too. Everyone wants to enjoy an interesting conversation. Make sure you are up on world news as well as industry news. Read a lot. Read books on your craft and just read great books. See a lot of films.

6. Be talented and hard working. As much as people say, "It is who you know," that is not the whole picture. Yes, you need people to mentor you. But they need to see that spark, that talent, that willingness to work hard before they will start recommending you to others and bringing you on to projects.

7. Overcome shyness. Try to be sociable and outgoing. It is not a field for wilting flowers. It is such a high-energy business that

(continues on next page)

INTERVIEW

Performing Arts Management (continued)

when people meet someone who is quiet and shy they think there is something wrong with them.

8. Be a good person. Hopefully you really are a good person, and you just have to let people see it. When you are working together over long hours people get to see how you handle stress, and whether you are loyal or if you backstab. Nothing can stay hidden.

9. Help. Help anyone you can and in every way you can. Who does not adore someone who makes their job easier? (Make sure, of course, that your job is under control before you wander off to help someone else.)

10. Ask questions. Show an interest in the business by asking a lot of questions. You will learn a lot and people will see your desire to learn and to get ahead. Just make sure you ask your questions at the right time. When your boss is cursing because an investor pulled out, it is not a good time to ask a question. Do not ask a question when they're trying to finish a scene before the sun goes down. Pay careful attention to the way people answer you. There are mentors out there for you, but not everyone you meet will want to guide you. Read the signs. If someone just wants you to do your job, if they look irritated when you ask why or how, then just do your job to the best of your ability. That person may not like teaching, but they may remember your competence when they're on another job and people are looking to hire.

rent. The flexible schedule leaves you time to stay home and write, work on a crew when you get a call, or go to an audition. Best of all, you can temp at a place where you may meet people who can help your career—a studio, a production company, an agency, a casting company. (See Chapter 6 for a list of temp agencies.) Your chances of being whisked from the "typing pool" to the executive suite on your first day are nil. But bosses do notice when temps have potential.

While you are word processing, you can ask your boss if he or she wants you to edit any letters. Some people may be offended, but most will be thrilled with the help and will soon start asking you to write the letter for them. By this time, they know you are not striving to be a secretary for life, and they will, hopefully, ask you about your career aspirations.

An alternative with all the above benefits except financial—and that is a big one—is to get an unpaid internship. You do not have to be a student to get an internship on a production crew or at a studio or network. During a tough economy, people tend to like free help. This can also be a way to be your reel, to move you up from that, "But what have you done?" level.

The Corporate World—Public Relations, Marketing, and Management

Are you interested in marketing movies? Do you think you have the knack to spot talent, to sense what will draw an audience and what will draw a yawn? The creative and development executive jobs at the studios are very competitive. The people who get these jobs think on their feet, think very fast, and are very smart. They are ambitious and determined. They have top notch social skills. But you need to put something on your résumé, preferably something that makes you shine, to get your foot in the door. That is where starting out in the corporate world can help, whether it is a marketing job at a corporation or a position at a public relations or ad agency. Get an entry level job, work as hard as you can, move up as fast as you can, and start working on your résumé. Although you may leave your corporate or agency job on a higher rung, you will probably start as an assistant at a studio. However, as described in the previous chapter, assistants do move up and they move up fast. You can learn a lot on the job at a PR or ad agency, but it will help to acquire some formal education in these fields. If you did not study any of this in school, consider working toward an MBA with a specialty in marketing or a degree in advertising or public relations during evenings while you work.

These companies and agencies can help you get started in the filmmaking end as well. Many corporations have in-house video departments where one or two people produce training programs themselves. Large hospitals and medical centers function similarly to corporations in that they often have in-house video and communications departments. Public relations agencies produce a lot of videos to promote clients and for fund-raising. Ad agencies, of course, produce commercials. In many cases, these companies contract with a small local production company to shoot and edit the publicity campaign or ad. But the writing is usually done at the agency, and people from the agency go on the shoot and watch the edit to make sure the final product is what they want.

With such high stakes, people in the film business are leery of unproven newcomers. Doing something to prove yourself, whether it is a great reel from film school or an early job in a closely related field, can be very helpful.

What If You Do Not Want to Relocate?

In spite of decentralization as a result of on-location filming, Hollywood is still the hub of the film industry, the site of all the major studios and media moguls. New York is a distant second. What if you are happy in Duluth? What if you are not ready to leave Portland? There can be benefits to starting out in Austin or Peoria or anywhere but Hollywood. The competition is less, obviously, and you will be able to move into bigger opportunities—full-length scripts for local theatrical events, leading roles for actors, or directing or producing—much faster than you will in Hollywood or New York. In a few years you can put together a pretty impressive list of credits and lose that dreaded "newcomer," "untested," "what if he or she screws up" label. There is probably work available in a reasonable driving distance—that is, less than two hours—from where you live. Regardless of your craft—production, writing, or acting—look at Variety411, which lists jobs according to category and city. Check the yellow pages for talent agencies, casting companies, and production companies. Contact the film commission in your state to find out what productions are scheduled. The film industry creates thousands of local jobs each year. You may be able to get a job on a Hollywood production filming on location in your area, or you may get work on local productions for theater groups, hospitals, corporations, and local ad and PR agencies. You may be so happy with this that in a few years you realize you have no desire to move. But if you do yearn to test the waters in Hollywood or New York, you will have an impressive list of credits and probably some contacts as well.

Professional
Ethics

To Tell or Not to Tell

Time was running out. They had to get the scene done today or crew overtime and extra acting days would break their budget. The director asked the cinematographer how fast he could light the next scene. He knew what the director wanted to hear. "Half hour, no problem." In fact, that was true. His gaffer could easily rig the lights in less time than that. But the cinematographer, who was more experienced than the director, knew that they would not be ready to shoot in an hour. He knew the painter had to paint the panel before they could rig the lights on it. He could truthfully tell the director, "Half hour," and then blame the set designer for not getting the set fixed in time. The director would look bad to the producer who had been on his back for cost overruns and delays. (The cinematographer thought he should have been the director on this film anyway; this guy was too inexperienced.) By the time the panels were painted the director would be screaming at the set designer. The producer would be screaming at the director. The cinematographer's crew would throw up the lights in record-breaking time. The overtime would be the fault of the set designer and the director.

The cinematographer did not go down this path. Instead, he used his experience to make a pretty good calculation of how long everything really would take, and he helped the director revise the schedule in a way that would allow them to wrap with a minimal amount of overtime. The film was a hit and came in pretty close to budget. The producer asked the cinematographer to direct his next picture. Filming is a team effort. When a film is a bust—in quality or budget—everyone looks bad. No one will say, "Oh, but the cinematography was great." If everything goes well people will want to work together again. Do the right thing because it is right. Chances are it will help your career.

Job-Specific Tips

Many of the tips that will help you get ahead in the film business are useful regardless what your specific career aspirations are. However, there are important tips for specific professions, which are discussed below.

Writers

One of the most difficult obstacles for a potential screenwriter to overcome is himself or herself. Most talented writers have deeply personal, thought-provoking tales to tell, statements they want to make, ideas they want to transmit. Studios and large production companies want to play it safe with something that seems to have a good chance of making it at the box office. Are these forces diametrically opposed? They are not. The studios, just like great writers from Shakespeare through Steinbeck, know that universal themes will draw and satisfy the largest audience. Once you have some successes under your belt, you may be able to convince a producer to take more of a risk with you. But first you have to achieve those successes. The good news is you do not have to sell out. You do not have to sit with a formula script and rewrite an age-old story. You just have to figure out a way to encase your story in a universal one. Films that accomplished this include *Casablanca, The Graduate, Schindler's List, Raging Bull, Midnight Cowboy, Rocky, Platoon*, and *Pulp Fiction*. Not bad. However, you cannot lose your voice. This may sound contradictory, but think about it. You are writing about the themes that great writers wrote about for hundreds of years, but from your point of view.

Struggling screenwriters spend a lot of time alone with a computer, and often become discouraged. It usually takes about five years for a screenwriter to sell a first script in Hollywood and ten years before he or she is recognized and has an ongoing flow of work, according to screenwriter Michael Lent. How do you not get discouraged during this frustrating period? In *Breakfast with Sharks*, Lent, who sold his first screenplay four years and nine months after arriving in Hollywood, encourages new writers to be patient, to be willing to write and rewrite, to pay attention to and learn from criticism, and to choose projects they feel passionate about. Remember, you are looking for universal themes, not rehashed stories. There is a difference.

It is important to make the first draft you send to your agent or to a producer as good as you can possibly make it. If the studio is interested they will still ask for rewrites to better reflect what they are looking for at the moment. But if you keep sending an agent scripts with flaws, they will get fed up. Many professional writers send their scripts to some trusted readers before submitting them to an agent or producer. Obviously, these should be readers who are knowledgeable about screenwriting and who will offer useful criticism.

Dealing with rejection is one of the most common and difficult aspects of being in the film business, one that plagues writers and actors. When you get a rejection, carefully scrutinize the criticism that comes with it. Learn from it. Allow yourself a few hours to sulk. Think of all the great writers who got tons of rejection letters, and move on.

What if you cannot convince an agent or producer to read your script? Producers and agents are more likely to review a script if you can tell them it placed near the top in a screenwriting competition. Producers and directors also attend many of the screenwriting competitions looking for talented new writers. Check out the screenwriting competitions listed in Chapter 6 and enter your script in as many as possible.

This will not be the first time you have heard this tip—write every day. It bears repeating. Some tips to help you succeed with this: Set aside a specific three-hour time period and do not answer the phone or play computer games during that time; when you are writing a first draft, write as fast as you, getting your scenario out as it flows; plan on rewrites to smooth it out and fine tune it. The other tip writers always hear is read, read, read. This is important for screenwriters, too, for obvious reasons. In addition, see movies, see movies, see movies.

Another tip, which can also help you support yourself, is to look for assignments writing low budget videos. These shows are usually not covered by the Writer's Guild and payment is lower than union scripts. The producer will appreciate it if you are sensitive to the budget by limiting the number of locations and the amount of computer-generated special effects.

Let's say you finally land a meeting with a producer or studio executive. Keep in mind that for all it took you to get in, you can be thrown out in seconds. That is why you need to be prepared to present your idea in stages. Start enthusiastically with a one-sentence concept. Make it a grabber. Move on to a three-minute rapid fire summary. If the producer asks questions (an excellent sign) keep your answers relatively brief. Continue to pitch by talking about characterization, plot, major themes, and, if relevant, why you wrote the story. If the producer still looks interested, continue to flesh out the story, giving as much information as you can to make the story compelling, but leave the producer wanting more—wanting to read your script.

Once you have a film or two to your credit, make sure you are the type of writer that producers and directors want to work with again. This means a writer with an open mind who is willing to listen to the director's suggestions for changes, willing to do rewrites, able to quickly solve scripting problems during filming, and able to meet deadlines.

Aspiring Actors

Get a job as a temp or clerk in a casting company, if you can. The perks are obvious—you meet people, you learn things—but the greatest advantage is what you learn that will help you face repeated rejection. Often, it is not about your acting. It is the crevice between what the director and producer envision and how they see you. Even though they have looked at your picture and read your credits, they do not really know whether they can picture you in the role until they actually see you. It is important to keep this in mind if you are going to stay sane in the sea of rejection faced by every actor.

Getting the part will depend primarily on whether you fit the director's image of your character and, of course, on your talent. But here are some tips to help you ace an audition and to make contacts for the next movie even if you do not get the part:

➜ Bring your head shots, résumé, and appointment book so that if they are interested in you, you can check your availability.

➜ Arrive at least 15 minutes before your scheduled appointment so you have time to calm down and prepare yourself mentally. You will sign in at the door, and sometimes people are seen in the order in which they arrive.

➜ Come prepared. You may be asked for a variety of performances. Sometimes you will be asked to demonstrate your range by performing two contrasting monologues (comedy and drama, for example). These should be under two minutes each. At some auditions, you will be given a small section of a script ("sides") and a short time to review it before being asked to deliver those lines. Occasionally you will be asked to improvise.

➜ Do not be too friendly with everyone else waiting to audition *if* you have been given "sides" or have a monologue prepared. Take the time to read the script and prepare.

Get into the character. It will be difficult to go from an animated waiting room conversation to the heart of a character when you are called into the audition. By the time you open the door to the audition room, you need to be the character.

→ Be polite. When you enter the room and are introduced to the people in the room, politely acknowledge each person.

→ Do it again, if you can. If you feel you messed up, ask if you may start again. Sometimes the director will refuse. If that is the case thank them politely, wish them well with the production, and say good-bye.

→ Dress. If you are not told about the character ahead of time or asked to wear a specific type of outfit, keep it simple and versatile. The typical casual Friday outfit of the corporate world works well: khaki pants or skirt, light blue blouse or shirt, blue sport jacket. Some actors dress all in black so that the outfit does not distract from their performance.

Some tips for when you are on the set or at home:

→ On the set, be an easy-to-be-around person. You have to be near the top to be temperamental (and tolerated), and even then it can backfire. So be nice, be punctual, and be prepared.

→ Off the set, keep your résumé and head shots up to date, take acting classes, read, and go to the movies. Read plays, movie scripts, and acting books in addition to whatever literature you love.

One of the great things about acting is that you can do it almost anywhere. There are talent agencies across the country. Producers are looking for actors for industrial and educational films, for small parts in a feature being filmed on location in your area, and for local theater. If you have not yet moved to Hollywood or New York, think about whether you would like to fine tune your craft and build credits in a less competitive environment. If you are already in Hollywood or New York, then you are surrounded by the energy of likeminded peers, and hopefully that will see you through the rough years.

Problem Solving

Decide Quickly, but Consider Everything

You are the producer. You are the one responsible for the schedule and for the budget. The director is ready to wrap and the weather channel is still predicting a 40 percent chance of rain for the next day, the day they had planned to shoot outside. What do you tell everyone about tomorrow's call?

You need to make a decision quickly. People are getting ready to leave. Think it through thoroughly but quickly. If you stay with the outside shoot and it rains, what will happen? Will everyone be drenched and miserable and cranky? Will there be shots you cannot get? What if it turns into a wasted day? On the other hand, there is a 60 percent chance it will not rain. If it does not rain, you will be on schedule and on budget. What will happen if you decide to revise the schedule and shoot inside tomorrow? Are all the necessary actors available? Do you have all the equipment you will need? Will you have to pay extra to keep today's talent until the day after tomorrow instead of letting them go tomorrow? How many will that be? How much? You have to take everything into consideration and then quickly—give it your best shot.

While you audition for acting parts, look into any job you can get on the set. You will make a lot of contacts and learn a lot about acting by working as a production assistant, for example. Temping at a studio or production company can help you make contacts.

Unions are very important in the acting profession. Even if you are yearning to act in film, you would be wise to take any acting job available—theater, television, or film—until you are established enough to earn a living in film alone. The three unions, described more thoroughly in Chapter 6, are:

→ Actor's Equity Association negotiates working conditions for stage actors. A percentage of non-Equity actors may work in Equity plays in "apprentice" positions. After you have performed in a certain number of plays you are eligible to join.

➡ Screen Actors Guild (SAG) negotiates for film and television actors. In order to join you must: get a cast position in a SAG film, TV show, or commercial; obtain vouchers while working as an extra; get a line while working as an extra; join AFTRA.

➡ American Federation of Television and Radio Actors (AFTRA) negotiates for TV and radio actors. Membership can also help you get into SAG, however. If you join AFTRA and work in a speaking part in an AFTRA project, SAG will allow you to join after one year of AFTRA membership.

The Path to Producer

Because you must know every area of the business to be a successful film producer, you can start in almost any position. Consider the enormous amount of time and effort you will have to put into any one package you bring to a studio. Packages generally include artwork (a sample of the poster that might advertise your film), an executive summary with biographies of key people, a treatment (prepared by the writer), cast and location suggestions, a complete marketing and distribution plan, production schedule, budget, and the legal and financial structure. You do not have time to usher through too many losers. You need to have a good idea of what the studio will want, of what will appeal to investors.

You need to be able to read a script the way the script reader in the story department will read it. You need to hire a director who will make it as you envision it—and on time and on budget. You need to know everyone's job.

As you go through the round of early jobs, you should let people you see as potential mentors know your ultimate goal. One of your first jobs should be as a script reader. You should also take a look at the "coverage" other script readers prepare on the incoming scripts. A job at a talent agency will teach you a lot and help you make contacts. If you can get in, the agency mailroom route discussed earlier could be very helpful to you. Finally, start looking for crew jobs on productions of various sizes. Work as a production assistant, a unit production manager, and a line producer. You might also try the assistant director route. As you think about each next position, think about what you have to learn and the contacts you need to make. Have you acquired sufficient knowledge of the business? Of how the studios work? Of dealing with investors? Do you know what makes a good script? Have you met writers, directors, and actors you might want to involve in your first production? If you have a lot of crew experience and you really know what it takes to put together a movie, you are only half way there. You need to know the studios inside out, have contacts with creative or development executives, and know which investors may be interested in your project before you take the leap. You may want to slowly put together your package while you are working at another job.

The Independent Producer

What if you see yourself as a filmmaker, an auteur, a writer/director/producer? What if you have a burning desire to tell a story, your story, your way? Some great films have been made by young filmmakers on low budgets, such as *Sex, Lies and Videotape*. There are many examples of films that do not make the radar but still make some money and bring tremendous satisfaction to their makers. Everyone anticipates and hopes that the growth of online distribution will help independent filmmakers generate an audience for their programs. Every year Sundance, the Tribeca Film Festival, and other festivals give birth to thought-provoking new voices. Some suggestions:

➡ Create a team: Try to form a collaborative team with other independent filmmakers, perhaps students from film school and people you meet at festivals or networking functions. Help each other on projects. When you are running camera or doing sound for a friend, you are getting experience and a credit and something for your demo reel.

➡ Go to festivals, premieres, and screenings to see what is out there and to meet people.

➡ Join IFP. This independent film producer's organization provides courses, mentors, and can even help you get funding to produce and distribute your film (see Chapter 6).

➡ Learn how to deal with investors. Though you may be more comfortable with other artists, they are probably no more able to finance your film than you are. You have to learn to be comfortable and converse with MBAs. When you are looking for money, you need to talk about the investor's potential return more than the benefit of your film to art or humanity.

➜ Know your audience. When you start a project, think very early on about your target audience. Many independent filmmakers are not looking for the mass-market appeal of a Hollywood movie, but you need a reasonably sized audience.

➜ Consider the world and how it may impact your product. Sometimes filmmakers are lucky. Who could predict the lawsuit against McDonald's would hit when *Supersize Me* was released? But if you have your finger on the pulse of society, you may be able to sense how trends and world events might impact the potential interest in your film.

Best Practice

Get It Done

Hoping to shine in the competitive environment of film, people strive for perfection. They seek to demonstrate their talent and skill. But you frequently hear directors and producers yell, "Good enough!" You need to find the right level of quality within the schedule and the budget. If the set can be lit with 100 lights, do not use 102. Consider whether the extra time you are taking to "make it better" will make a visible difference to anyone other than you. "Think of Thoreau," suggests Frank Prinzi, A.S.C, "simplify, simplify, simplify...Simplicity of life and elevation of purpose." Keep it simple. Get it done.

When you have a script, start sending it to screenwriter contests. This may help you find a distributor. When you have a film, begin to enter it in festivals. Most important, give yourself time. This is truly an area where people become overnight successes after ten years of struggle.

Postproduction: Editing, Visual Effects, and Sound

The editor, the director, and the writer play the three most significant roles in the impact of the film. Writers see the editor as the one who does the final rewrite of their script. Directors understand how crucial the editor's role is to carrying out their vision—many directors insist on working with specific editors, some with only one particular editor. It is not surprising that the editors share directors' love of film. If you think you might be interested in editing, ask yourself: Do I thrive on the excitement of the set or do I prefer the more solitary analytical process of editing? Ray Hubley, a feature film and documentary film editor (*Dead Man Walking, Who is Norman Lloyd?*) says, "For me, solving a problem editorially and discovering the chemistry that occurs when you construct a whole from pieces is more exciting than anything I've seen on a sound stage."

The best way to break into editing is to get an unpaid internship. If you need income, consider dividing your time between paid work and an internship. During an internship you will get the experience necessary to decide whether or not editing is for you. "I meet many young people nowadays with an interest in editing," says Hubley. "The light in the eyes of a real acolyte is unmistakable." Chances are if you feel the passion and the editor for whom you intern sees that light, you will have found a mentor. If you are sure about your passion but you do not connect with a particular editor, look for another internship.

Many successful editors are not film-school graduates. You can take courses to learn the necessary software while you continue to learn the art from your mentor. At some point, your mentor may be able to offer you a paid assistant editor position or refer you to a colleague who has an assistant position available.

When you meet the people who work in sound, both postproduction and production, you will find a common denominator—most of them have been fascinated by the manipulation of sound since childhood. Some are professional musicians; most love music. Try to get a job as a sound trainee in a postproduction house. If you cannot, try for a runner or any type of work in a post house. Alternatively, look into an unpaid internship. In sound, most people do indeed start at the bottom and work up, often with two to three years in each position—learning on the job is really the only good way to learn.

Many people who are interested in visual effects or animation—both are computer generated graphics—have degrees in fine arts. If so, your college portfolio will help you get a job or at least an internship. If you do not have a portfolio, try to get work that will enable you to build a portfolio—graphics jobs at magazines or for public relations or advertising companies, for example. Keep in mind that to pursue a career in this area you need artistic talent, computer skills, and a lot of patience. This work will keep you glued to the computer for many hours, tweaking tiny details to achieve the effect you desire. An unpaid internship or, with luck, a paid apprentice-ship, is a good next step. This is the fastest growing field in the film industry and there will be a lot of opportunity for people with the right skills.

Director

Many people who love film yearn for the opportunity to direct. Many famous actors and writers with no need of additional income want to direct. Flanked by the writer and editor, the director is the person whose vision is best reflected in any film. If you are a writer, there is nothing more satisfying than directing your own work, car-rying your vision from idea to film.

Directors need to know the process inside-out in order to achieve the impact they want. What camera angle, what lighting, what set design will make the audience see the character's anguish and feel empathy for her? The director knows how to pull together all the creative elements to achieve the desired impact on the audience. Directors therefore need considerable technical knowledge about lights, camera, and sound as well as creativity to achieve the look they want. Directors also must have excellent interpersonal skills. Although you hear about the egotistical directors stomping off the set with the producer frantically following behind, more often the director is the one cajoling the actors to get the effect he or she wants. The director strives to get the best possible performance from every actor. If it is early in your career, and you know this is what you want to do, there are a number of paths. Similar to the producer, the director's breadth of knowledge must be so wide that you can start in almost any position. Any job on a crew or in post will do. The Direc-tor's Guild, in conjunction with the Alliance of Motion Picture and Television Producers, offers an exemplary assistant director training program. "If you really want to direct, you need to start writing," advises Frank Prinzi, A.S.C. Ultimately, jobs on the camera and lighting ends will be most beneficial. A job as a cinematographer or director of photography is a good jumping off point to directing.

The Crew

If you love sound and are interested in doing sound on production, following the path above to do sound in post is a good way to start. When you have several years of experience in postproduction sound, you can start asking producers and directors for the opportunity to work on the set. You will meet many producers and directors while you are doing post.

Many gaffers and grips come from families of gaffers and grips. But if this interests you, a good way to make contacts is by working as a production assistant. You should also take some courses for electricians. The IATSE union can give you additional tips on getting started.

Production Design, Set Design, Art Director, and Scenic Design

These are jobs for varying types of artists. Building a portfolio with related work is the best way to get your foot in the door. It will be to your advantage if you have experience in interior design, architecture, or graphic arts. Interning or working in summer stock or local theater is one of the best ways to learn the craft and to develop

Fast
Facts

Oscar Trivia

- The first Academy Awards ceremony was held in the Blossom Room of the Hollywood Roosevelt Hotel on May 16, 1929; 270 people attended.
- Over 2,700 gold-plate Oscar statuettes have been awarded.
- The actor to receive the most Oscar nominations: Jack Nicholson (12 nominations).
- Two films to receive the most nominations: *All About Eve*, 1950 (14 nominations); *Titanic*, 1997 (14 nominations).
- The only American woman to receive a best director award: Kathryn Bigelow, *The Hurt Locker* (2010).
- Eight foreign language films to receive a best picture nomination: *Grand Illusion* (1938), *Z* (1969), *The Emigrants* (1972), *Cries and Whispers* (1973), *The Postman* (1995), *Life is Beautiful* (1998), *Crouching Tiger, Hidden Dragon* (2000), *Letters from Iwo Jima* (2006).

an impressive portfolio. After you garner theater experience, try to get a job as a production assistant and follow around the people in production and set design whenever you have a free moment. Ask questions. Offer to help—when it does not detract from your PA responsibilities. Ask if you can help the designers on your days off.

How to Find Out About Jobs

You have undoubtedly picked up that the theme of this chapter is mentoring and networking, and these are definitely the best ways to find out about upcoming jobs and to increase your chance of getting a job when one does come up.

You do not want to sit and wait, however. If you want to work on the set, consider your mayor as a possible job recruiter. Producers have to obtain a permit from the mayor's office before they begin to shoot in a city, and the mayor's office will list film jobs on its Web site. Similarly you can contact the film commission in your state. (A growing number of states—but not every state—have film commissions.) The *Ross Report* and the *Hollywood Reporter* also publish lists of films about to go into production. Post your résumé wherever you can, with the professional associations and guilds and on Web sites. If you are hoping to obtain a job as an assistant at a studio, you will probably have to go through an employment agency unless someone is recommending you for a position. Call the employment agencies and find out which ones have the studios as clients.

Making a Good First Impression

In most fields, people warn that you have a short time to make a good first impression on a job interview. In film, you need to cut that time in half. You may have minutes. What is considered a good first impression depends somewhat on the job. Talent agencies are looking for high energy, over-confident, and somewhat aggressive employees. Being a bit "cocky" may work to your advantage. Not so on the movie set. If you are hoping to move up through the ranks by starting as a PA, the producer wants to be assured that you thoroughly know what you are doing and that you will do it. You need to briefly but impressively detail what you have done that demonstrates that you know what will be expected of you on the set. This has less to do with showing your creativity on a student production and more to do with knowing how a film crew operates. You should know the names of all the equipment. You need to show that you understand and will perform the role of the PA: that you are hardworking, energetic, and eager to do anything you are asked to help the production. Even though you may aspire to greater things, right now people want to know that you will do the menial things with a smile. "Tomorrow" you may be a hot shot director, but today you are a PA. Your career goals take second seat to your desire to help facilitate the production by doing whatever is necessary, from getting coffee to lugging equipment to running after extras. If a producer questions you about your film school background, for example, you might reply: "Yes, I do hope to direct someday, but right now I want to be the best PA, I want to do exactly what you need." People are going to be leery of recent film school graduates who either eschew "menial" work or are so eager to learn that they distract everyone else with their questions.

Two Final Tips

One characteristic that differentiates people who succeed from those who do not is persistence. This holds true for any career. People embarking on a career in film often have to be persistent for a longer period of time, however, than those in other fields. It is easy to become discouraged in the time it takes to obtain a satisfying job in film, a job that you feel uses some of your abilities. It is not easy to trudge along as a PA when former schoolmates are rising up the ladder in corporate jobs. Many people "drop out" of film to become accountants and lawyers. A lot depends on how desperately you want it, how deeply you love it. People who have succeeded in film, whether it be as a writer, a director, or an actor, will tell you that this is "in their blood" (even though it is not in their family). They have been fiddling around in some aspect of film since childhood. This is what they have always wanted. It is the love of film, not the desire for success or celebrity that sustains the people who make it. Introspection will help you get through the difficult early years. Think about your childhood, about the things in life that have brought you pleasure. If you truly love film, if you have always loved film, remember that when the going gets rough. Having a five-year plan can help keep you motivated. Make up a timetable with the successes you hope to achieve each year. You can vary this plan as unforeseen events cause you to consider something different. You may know that you have always loved film, but until you are working in the business, you may not know which area of film is most satisfying to you, and in which area you seem to have the most talent and ability.

Finally, remember to pass it on. You do not have to be at the top of your career to help others. Share what you know with others. When you hear about an upcoming event of interest, e-mail your friends and colleagues. When there is finally someone more junior than you on the set, start mentoring. It is sort of like that saying about love, "To keep it, you have to give it away."

The most important tip for success emphasized in this chapter is the importance of finding people who will help you. Networking is the crucial path, finding a mentor is the ultimate goal. The economic stakes are high in film and people want experience. The only way they are going to ease up on their experience requirement is with the assurance of a trusted colleague who can vouch for you. Networking also means maintaining the personal skills, the character and personality attributes that make you someone people want to help. Of course you need talent and ability. That is a given. But you need to be a nice person with good character who can be trusted. You need to be interesting, personable, and social so that people want to get to know you enough to see that good character. In your early jobs, you have to put your career aspirations in the back of your mind—not out of your mind, but in the back—and concentrate on doing the job at hand. People will recommend you from one producer to another or from one corporate executive to another if you did a great job as a PA or an assistant, not because you have laudable career goals. On the other hand, keep those goals in the back of your mind and continually reflect on whether you are on path. If you start out working as a PA because you want to direct and you find your interest is really in the business end, start looking for assistant jobs in the studio.

Chapter 5

Talk Like a Pro

Many business professionals can recount stories from their early years, when crew members had a good laugh at their expense. Many can also recall some serious moments, such as when they really could not figure out what a producer wanted. This glossary is intended to spare you as many of those moments as possible. Mark the words that pertain to what you are doing now, and memorize them. If you hear a term on the set, look it up as soon as you get home.

above-the-line expenses The film expenses committed to prior to production, such as paying the scriptwriter, salaries for producer, director, and cast.

The Academy Although best known for the Academy Awards (the Oscars), the Academy of Motion Picture Arts and Sciences (AMPAS) is also heavily involved in education and research activities.

action When the director yells "action," it is the actors' cue to begin performing.

actors, cast Actors with lines.

actors, extras or background Actors without lines or a specific role. The extras are the people in crowd scenes in a movie.

actor's call The time an actor is to arrive on the set. The assistant director will arrange a "call time," which will be a minimum of one hour before performance time. It is a good idea for an actor to arrive even earlier than this to become accustomed to the set and to achieve the right frame of mind for the character.

adaptation   A script that is written (adapted) from a finished written version of the story. Films may be adapted from novels or from theatrical performances.

advertising   The advertising manager and the promotion manager work closely with the marketing manager in an effort to generate as large an audience as possible for the film. The advertising manager focuses on advertisements placed in print and broadcast media.

against   A partial payment for a script or property. That payment is "against" the total payment agreed upon in the contract.

agent   A person who represents an actor, writer, or director. The agent tries to get work for the person and in exchange receives 10 percent of the money the person earns.

American Federation of Television and Radio Artists (AFTRA)   This is a union that has some reciprocity with SAG.

American Society of Cinematographers (ASC)   This is a professional association with international membership.

animator/visual effects artists   Also called multimedia artists, animators and visual effects artists use computers to create images, moving characters, and visual effects. *See* CGI.

apple box   Used during filming, a camera operator or piece of equipment can be raised by putting it on this wooden box.

art department   Often the largest department on any production, the art department includes all those who design and create the visual elements of sets.

art director   Designs graphics which will be used in the sets.

aspect ratio   A measure of the relative sizes of the horizontal and vertical components of an image.

assistant camera operator   The first assistant focuses and handles exposure; the second assistant backs up the first and runs to get whatever is needed, such as additional lenses or film; the third assistant keeps the camera filled with fresh film. The third assistant is often in the darkroom during filming.

assistant director   The first assistant director (first AD) works closely with the line producer to set call times for talent and crew and to make sure the production schedule is followed. The second assistant director reports to the first AD and prepares and distributes daily paperwork, such as call sheets, production reports, and SAG contracts.

Association of Film Commissions International (AFCI)   Film commissions from different countries belong to the AFCI. The film commissions offer incentives to U.S. filmmakers wishing to film on location in their country, and they help guide filmmakers to local resources.

attached Refers to a situation in which a famous actor or director has expressed interest in or committed to a project. This can help the producer get backing for a project and it is a selling point to the studio.

audio recording engineers Also called sound effects editors, they manipulate different parts of the sound track during post-production—the dialogue, music, and background sound—to fit the picture.

auteur Refers to a director who creates a film that reflects his or her personal vision or worldview. The auteur director controls all aspects of the filmmaking process, from script, through production and edit, so that the film is distinctly and thoroughly his or her vision.

automated dialogue replacement editor Also known as ADR dialogue editor or ADR mixer (and formerly known as the dubbing editor), this person makes sure the best audio is used for each scene. When the ADR cannot find a suitable take, he or she re-records the actor in a sound studio. ADR may also refer to audio that was re-recorded and dubbed in to replace audio that was recorded on location.

AVID Manufacturer of a popular nonlinear editing system. Competitors include Lightworks and Apple's FinalCut Pro.

background The actors working as "extras" or "background."

background artist Better known as "scenic artist" or "matte artist," this person designs or constructs the art placed at the rear of a set. Also called scenic artist or matte artist.

backlot An undeveloped area on studio property that may be used for constructing large open-air sets or filming wilderness scenes.

barndoors Blinders on the side of lights to keep the light from going everywhere.

barney Quilted piece put on the camera to reduce camera noise.

beat sheet An abbreviated outline or blue print for a script, the beat sheet is broken down into acts and includes a brief description of each scene. It can be used to break down the scene for the different actors—that is, the "beats" for actors.

below-the-line expenses Those expenses not included above the line, such as costs of materials, music rights, and publicity.

Everyone Knows

Slang on the Set

Here are some terms you will hear on the set but you will not find in a glossary.

Abby Singer   The next to the last shot of the day. Named for Abby Singer, a renowned production manager. When he showed up on a set he always said, "Next shot is a martini."

Martini shot   The last shot of the day, suggesting that the next shot will be in a glass.

Baby   A 1,000 watt (1K) light with a focused lens

Blonde   A 2,000 watt (2K) tungsten light

Redhead   A 1,000 watt (1K) tungsten light

best boy grip   As assistant to the key grip, the best boy grip takes care of the equipment and recruits additional crew manpower when needed.

billing   The way the names are listed in credits and advertisements, including size and position.

biopic   Biographical film or television movie.

blimp   Fiberglass housing for the camera to reduce camera noise.

blind commitment   This is when a studio makes a deal with a producer, director, writer, or actor to develop a new project with them following the success of a current project. This is a reward for the successful project and a way of maintaining exclusivity on their talent.

blue screen   Actors are filmed in front of a blue background, which is then replaced by chromakeying in postproduction. The blue screen has largely been replaced by a green screen.

boom   A large microphone on the end of a long stick. The boom operator holds the mic above the area being filmed and moves it from person to person as they speak.

boom operator The boom operator works for the sound engineer and handles the boom mic during filming, moving it from person to person. The boom mic is a fairly large microphone on the end of a long pole.

bootleg An illegal, pirated version of a movie.

bounce card To obtain soft, indirect lighting a white or silver card is used to bounce the light.

box office Gross or total amount of money paid by viewers in theaters.

breakdown script List of everything needed for each scene, such as actors and props.

break it When someone other than the director needs to have filming stop for any reason. For example, the sound mixer may yell, "break it" if the sound is unclear and the microphones need to be adjusted. The actor may yell "break it" if he or she is about to sneeze.

bump A meeting that is rescheduled at the last minute. Studio executives will always give priority to projects already in production. If you have a meeting scheduled to pitch a new project or script, you will often get "bumped" if a producer or director of a project needs to meet with the studio executive.

call Sequence of directions at the beginning of filming—such as "Roll sound," "roll camera," "mark it," "action."

call sheet List of which actors are needed for each scene and the time they are needed on the set.

call time The time that each member of cast and crew must be on the set.

camera operator/A and B cameras The camera operator focuses and moves the camera to achieve the shots called for by the director or director of photography. Cameras are identified by letters—A and B, followed by additional letters if there are more cameras. The director will say, for instance, "Camera A, wide shot of room." "Camera B, close up of actor."

camera ready Refers to a completed and adequately revised script that is ready to be filmed.

cast contingent When a studio or investor commits to financing or producing a project based on specific casting. *See* attached.

casting director Breaks down the script according to role and arranges auditions.

cel animation This is the way animation was done before the 1990s, but it has been almost completely replaced by computer generated animation. In cel animation, images are hand drawn, transposed to plastic sheets, each with a different element of a scene.

CGI Computer generated imagery is the creation of 3D visual effects with the computer. It is used for animation and special effects.

change pages Pages of script that have been edited during filming. Sometimes the script writer is asked to revise upcoming scenes. These change pages are given to the actors and crew to replace the original scenes.

character arc The way a character develops throughout the story—he or she becomes more insightful, or more understanding of another character or event, for example.

cheat Cheating is when the director asks an actor to assume a physical pose that would be unnatural in real life but will create a realistic perspective on film. For example, sometimes an actor is asked to look away from the person to whom he or she is speaking and at an object in the background. When the scene is shot, however, it will appear that the actor is looking directly at the other person. Sometimes props are also put in "unnatural" positions because they look better for the camera.

chopsocky A martial arts film.

chromakeying Color elements (chroma) are replaced with different picture elements. In other words, the character is filmed in front of a blue or green screen and then superimposed on another background. (*See* blue screen *and* green screen.)

chyron Type used on the screen.

cinematographé All-in-one camera, printer, and projector invented by the Lumiére brothers in 1895.

cinematographer *See* director of photography.

cinema vérité A documentary in which the director films things as they are.

Classification and Ratings Administration (CARA) Under the Motion Picture Association of America (MPAA), CARA is the organization that rates films.

claymation Animation of clay or plasticine constructed models.

close-up This is a camera shot in which the person or object the camera is pointed at fills the frame. When used to refer to a person (that is, a close-up of an actor) this is a shot of the face and sometimes neck. When used to refer to something other than the face, this may be a part of the body, such as wringing hands or a tapping foot, or an object, such as a gun or a part of a book that fills the frame.

code numbers   Numbers on the tape used to identify scenes and facilitate the edit. For example, the editor knows that scene 1, take 3, is located at a certain numbered code. (*See* time code.)

cold reading   At an audition an actor may be asked to give a reading with material he or she has not seen before and therefore not rehearsed. The casting agent gives the actor "sides" a few minutes before the audition. *See* sides.

color temperature   The color of light sources. A high color temperature is associated with bluer light; a low color temperature with yellow light.

consider   When the script reader's report or coverage of your script is marked "consider" it is in between a "pass" and a recommendation that the studio higher-ups read it. It generally means the script reader had a favorable impression of your script but has some reservations.

continuity   The process of making a scene seamless as different shots are used. For example, there is a person in charge of continuity on the set who makes sure that if a particular actor is wearing glasses on the wide shot, he is also wearing glasses on the close up.

cookie   A flat board with irregular holes used to create a pattern of shadows when put in front of a light.

costume designer   Researches appropriate clothing for the period of the film and either purchases or rents costumes or has them made.

coverage   After a script reader for the studio reviews a submitted script, he or she attaches a report that is called "coverage." Coverage includes a synopsis of the script and a detailed report on what the reader thought about various elements. As a writer, you can learn and perfect your craft by paying attention to these comments.

crane shot   The camera is elevated on a crane in order to show the scene from above.

creative exec (CE)   A middle management studio executive, the CE reviews scripts recommended by the script reader. If the CE likes the script he or she will consult with upper management about purchasing or optioning it. The CE may then oversee the development of the project, offering the writer feedback and suggestions for changes or rewrites. Sometimes CEs are called development execs (DEs).

C-stand   A type of light stand with fixed legs which can swing in and out.

cut   On the set, "cut" is the director's order to stop shooting a scene. The director is the only one who will yell "cut" on the set. If anyone else—assistant director, sound mixer, actor, or camera operator—needs to stop the scene for any reason, they will yell "break it." In editing, a cut is the basic transition from one shot to another with no time lapse effect (dissolve) or other special effect. For example, the editor may "cut" from a wide shot to a close up of someone in the same scene at the same time.

cutaway   A shot from a different camera angle that can be helpful in editing. For example, if you are shooting a wide shot of people at a meeting, you will shoot some takes of close-ups of individuals at the meeting and maybe of a blackboard or other prop at the meeting. These are cutaways. In post, the editor can use cutaway shots to arrange takes.

dailies   Rushes returned the same day. (*See* rushes.)

day-for-night   A shot done during the day but made to look like night.

deal memo   A contractual agreement that outlines specific terms between the writer and the studio, such as what the writer will write, the due date, and what the studio will pay.

demographics, or "demos"   A way of describing the target audience for a film by age and gender.

depth of field   As the camera focuses on one object, depth of field refers to the areas in focus in front and behind that object.

development   The phase prior to a go-ahead to produce a film when the producer ushers a package through the studio hoping to get a green light. The package contains an outline of the idea or a script, along with tons of information suggesting why this will be a good deal for the studio.

development hell   This term is used when, over a prolonged period of time, various people at the studio ask for more information or script rewrites prior to deciding whether or not to purchase the property.

diffusion   A filter used on the camera to create a soft focus effect; or, a white or pearlescent piece of material used on a light to soften shadows.

digital editing   Electronically altering or combining images.

digital video disc (DVD)   Discs that can store video.

director   The director's vision brings the script to life. The director is in charge of all creative matters. The director has the final say on talent, location choice, casting, set design, costumes, music, and everything that will impact the look and feel of the production. The director works with the actors to elicit their best performances and he or she works with the director of photography and set designer to make sure the film reflects his or her vision.

director of photography   The DOP, or cinematographer, works closely with the director and figures out how to photograph in a way that reflects the director's vision. This means orchestrating camera framing, lighting, and so forth. The DOP heads the camera and lighting teams.

director's cut   A fully-edited cut of the movie but one that has not been color corrected or had all sound elements mixed. The director is allowed six weeks to complete a cut of the movie without any studio interference.

Directors Guild of America (DGA)   This is the union and professional association for directors and assistant directors.

dissolve   One way the editor transitions from one scene to the next in post. A dissolve is when one scene is slowly fading out as the next scene is fading in.

distribution   The sale and licensing of a film to a variety of outlets, including theaters, television stations, and retailers. The distribution company works closely with marketing to identify a target audience for a film and to develop the best strategy to roll it out, including determining time of year for release, whether to release to a few theaters or nationwide at once, and when to make it available on DVD.

docudrama   A drama based on fact that includes fictional elements.

documentary   A nonfiction narrative with real people, not actors.

dolly grip   Dollies are platforms on which you put a camera when you want to shoot from above. The dolly has a hydraulic arm that lowers and raises the platform. The dolly grip maintains the dollies and makes sure they are where they are needed.

dope sheet   A list of scenes that have been filmed.

downloading   A type of IPTV in which the entire film is transmitted to the computer in one piece.

dramedy   A film that has elements of both drama and comedy.

dresser   A wardrobe assistant who helps actors with their costumes.

dubbing   In post, dubbing is when an actor is re-recorded in the sound studio to replace poor quality sound. *See* ADR.

Dutch tilt   A camera composition on a diagonal. Also called a "canted angle."

edge numbers   The tiny numbers on the edge of film.

editing   During postproduction the editor selects the best takes for each scene and puts them together in a way that that optimizes the director's vision. Some say the editor does the final script "rewrite." Many directors have a limited number of editors with whom they will work.

establishing shot   The first shot in a new location that orients the audience to the site. An establishing shot is generally a wide shot.

executive producer   Supervises several producers. An executive position primarily concerned with finances.

exhibition   The places where a movie is shown including theaters, broadcast and cable television, the Internet, and stores that sell or rent DVDs.

extreme close-up (ECU)   Very tight face shot in which the subject appears larger than the frame. Usually part of the top of the face is cut off.

fade   A transition used in editing where a scene fades to black. Fade out refers to a scene gradually changing to black. Fade in refers to a scene that gradually goes from black to the image.

fake shemp   An actor who has no lines and whose face is not seen either because of heavy makeup or the camera angle. The term comes from an actor used to finish the Three Stooges films after Shemp Howard's death.

feature   A full-length film, generally running between 90 minutes and 2 hours.

film buyer   Someone who purchases films from a distributor on behalf of an exhibitor.

film festival   A contest in which multiple films are judged. There are thousands of festivals worldwide, some geared to specific types of films, and some more prestigious than others. Entering a film in a festival is an opportunity to attract a distributor as well as a chance to win a prize.

film noir   This genre refers to detective films showing seedy locations, dark brooding characters, and corruption.

filter   Tinted glass or plastic put in front of the camera lens to change the color rendition of the shot.

financing   Raising money to produce a film, usually from multiple investors.

first-look deal   This is an arrangement between an individual (usually a very successful writer, producer, director, or actor) and a studio or production company. The individual pledges to bring all new ideas or concepts to that studio first, allowing the studio executive to say yes or no before bringing the proposed project to another studio. Studios often engage producers and others in these first-look deals by offering them perks, such as free office space or covering the cost of their overhead.

flag   Large black cloth on a frame used to keep light out of a part of the shot.

flare   When light strikes the camera lens and makes the image foggy.

flashback   A scene that depicts events occurring in the past.

flash frame   A single clear frame between two shots.

flatbed   Used in film editing, a flatbed looks like a large desk with a screen across from the chair. Most editing is now done digitally, so flatbeds are not often used.

Foley editor   During postproduction, Foley editors add the subtle sounds that microphones often miss during production—the rustling of clothes, or soft footsteps for example. He or she also enhances major sound effects like explosions or car crashes.

footage   The amount of film shot in a day. Also used to refer to the raw film before it is edited.

foot candle   A measurement of light.

forced perspective   By using objects of different sizes and placed a varying distances, an area is made to look larger than its true size.

frame   An individual picture image.

freeze frame   An optical effect created in post to make it look like all action has stopped.

gaffer   The gaffer, or chief lighting technician, is head of the electrical department and is responsible to the DOP for lighting design and set up. The gaffer selects the type of lights for a scene and decides where to place them. The term gaffer comes from the early days of film when stagehands controlled natural light with large tent cloths on long poles, called gaffs.

gel   A thin, tinted plastic-like sheet placed over a light to change the color of the projected light. If someone assigns you to "cleansing the gels," tell them gels can't be cleansed. This is an experienced crew's way of teasing a novice crew member.

generator   Also called Genny, the generator is sometimes brought on location to provide electricity.

giraffe A mechanically extendable boom mic.

godfather A mentor who is willing to make phone calls on your behalf

green light A go ahead to begin production on a script.

green screen A green screen serves the same purpose as a blue screen, but is, obviously, green and is considered more sensitive than a blue screen. Today, most directors use a green screen, rather than a blue screen. *See* blue screen.

greensman Crew member who obtains, places, and maintains any vegetation used on the shoot.

grip A skilled crew member responsible for set up, adjustment, and maintenance of production equipment on the set. The grip may assist with camera movement, lighting and rigging. In the United Kingdom, grip refers to someone who works only with the equipment on which the camera is mounted.

halation Effect occurs when bright areas of the image appear to softly bleed at the edges.

hardtop Slang for a movie house.

head room Space between top of person's head and top of frame.

heat When you are hot you are hot. This refers to a script or project (or a person) of great interest in the filmmaking community. A hot property usually means several studios will bid on the project thereby raising the price. When an actor, director, or writer has just completed a successful commercial project, they say he or she "has heat."

high concept An idea that sound very marketable, one that seems to have blockbuster potential.

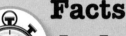

Fast Facts

Four Facts about Golden Globe Awards

- The Golden Globes are awards in both motion pictures and television.
- They are sponsored by the Hollywood Foreign Press Association (HFPA).
- From Golden Globe Awards, the HFPA has donated more than $8.4 million over the past 14 years to entertainment-related charities and scholarship funds.
- The HFPA represents publications in 55 countries with a combined readership of over 250 million.

hit your mark   When the actor finds where he or she is to be in the scene without looking at the marks that have been placed on the floor.

HMI   A halogen metal incandescent light is a very bright, power-efficient light that is balanced for the color temperature of daylight.

HOD   Head of department. May refer to coordinators.

Hollywood Ten   Directors and writers who stood up to the House Un-American Activities Committee in the early 1950s and refused to give names of colleagues who "might" have had anything to do with the Communist Party. The Hollywood Ten endured jail time and years of being blacklisted.

honeywagon   Mobile dressing room for actors, used on location. Honeywagons also contain portable bathrooms for cast and crew. (Usually a trailer.)

hot set   This is a finished set where all the furniture and props have been placed and are ready for filming. It is important not to move anything on a hot set.

incident light reading   A measurement of light hitting a subject obtained using a light meter.

independent   A film made outside the studio system or a production company that operates outside the studio system.

indie   Short for *independent.*

industrial or educational film   A film that will shown in nontheatrical outlets to a discrete audience.

insert shot   A close up of some detail or object in the scene that the editor can cut away to in post.

International Alliance of Theatrical Stage Employees, Moving Picture Technicians, Artists, and Allied Crafts (IATSE)   This is the union representing most people in the industry, excluding actors, writers, directors, and producers.

intertitles   A title card that is intercut with a scene. This was used primarily during the silent era to help viewers follow the action.

IPTV Internet Protocol TV (IPTV)   Transmission of a film directly into the home via the Internet.

jib   The arm of a mechanical crane.

judder   Instability in picture that may occur when images at one frame rate are converted to a different frame rate for viewing.

jump cut   In editing and in the finished film, the scene will appear to jump if the editor were to put together two takes of a scene (to get the best lines from each take) that used the same shot. In order to cut takes of the same scene together they must be at different camera angles. *See* pick up.

K   May be used as an abbreviation for kilowatts or for Kelvin.

kelvin   Color temperature scale.

key costumer   Assists the costume designer in procuring costumes.

key grip   The key grip is responsible to the DOP and the gaffer for providing and placing all diffusion and for moving, setting up, and striking and transporting lights.

kinetograph   First moving picture camera. Invented by Thomas Edison.

kinetoscope   Invented by Edison and used when movies could only be seen as peep shows. This is a cabinet in which a continuous loop of film played while a viewer looked in through a small hole.

layout   Also known as blocking, this refers to determining where everything and everyone—camera, lights, actors, and so on—should be prior to filming.

layout artist   Plots every shot whether live footage or computer generated.

lead character technical director   In an animated film the lead character technical director oversees a team of character technical directors and works with the lead artist to make sure the animation works and flows.

leadman   Also referred to as "lead person." A member of the art department who works for the set decorator.

legs   They say "a movie has legs," when it has been out awhile and is continuing to reap large box-office returns.

letterboxing   When you see a film on television and it has a black border on top and bottom, it is "letterboxed." This is done to transfer from film to video, which has a different aspect ratio, without cutting off the film image.

lighting board operator   Works at a console and controls the level and intensity of lights on the set.

lined script   During filming, the script supervisor prepares a "lined script," showing which scenes have been shot.

line producer   Figures the budget, breaking it down to a daily basis, and organizes the process of production in the most cost-effective way.

lip sync   Sound that is synchronized to the picture so that the person's lips move the way the audio sounds.

live area   The image you see in the camera viewfinder that will actually be recorded on the film stock. The area around the live area, the safe area, will not show.

location manager   The person who handles issues, such as obtaining permits, relating to the location in which you are shooting.

location scout   A person who looks for good places to film.

location sound   Also called "production sound," this is any sound obtained during filming, whether it is the sync sound of dialogue or wild sound.

lock it down   When you hear the assistant director yell, "lock it down," that is everyone's cue to be quiet and move out of frame because filming is about to begin. Right after the AD calls, "lock it down," the camera operator will call, "speed," indicating that shooting can begin.

log line   A one or two sentence summary of a story (from an idea, script, or book).

long shot   A camera angle that shows a person's entire body rather than just the head (close up) or the head and shoulders (medium shot). A long shot generally includes some of the background environment. Can also refer to a distant shot where the characters appear small against the background.

look development lead   Also known as a "lookdev," this person works in computer generated graphics and liaises with those responsible for modeling, concept art, and other effects.

low-concept   An idea or script targeted to a limited audience. Difficult to sell to a major studio.

Macguffin   Also known as "weenie" and coined by Alfred Hitchcock, *Macguffin* refers to something in the film that the actors know is very important but of which the audience is not yet aware.

magazine   Light proof chamber(s) attached to camera to hold film.

magic hour   The very short period around sunrise and sunset when light levels are changing quickly.

majors   The six primary Hollywood studios—Universal, Sony, Paramount, Disney, Warner Bros, and 20th Century Fox.

manager   Some actors, writers, and directors have a manager as well as an agent. The manager focuses on the person being represented, advising him or her on ways to improve a script, productions that will benefit their image, and other issues. While the agent is concerned primarily with the sale, the manager is concerned with the person and the development of his or her career. The manager also takes 10 percent of what the person earns, on top of the agent's 10 percent.

mark   On the set, a piece of tape is affixed to the floor to show an actor where to stand.

marketing   The marketing manager works closely with the distribution manager and oversees the promotion and advertising managers to ensure a coordinated effort to draw an audience. The marketing strategy is the overall plan that will be followed in different ways in promotion and advertising. This strategy will identify a target audience, create an image or message for the film, and make sure all advertising and promotion reflects that image.

matte artist   Also called the "mattematician" or the "scenic artist," this artist creates artwork for the background of a shot.

M&E   Music and effects.

medium shot   Shows the character from the waist up.

method acting   The actors draw upon personal emotions and experiences in order to better understand and portray their characters. Sometimes, actors arrange to have experiences similar to those of their character. This style of acting is associated with the approach designed by the Russian actor and director Constantin Stanislavsky, and is sometimes called the "Stanislavsky system."

mise-en-scene   The total of all the factors that influence the look and feel of a scene. ("What's put into the scene.")

mix   During postproduction, all sound tracks are combined during a mix.

modeler   Person who uses computer graphics to develop a 3D character or object.

MOS   When the director calls "MOS" (and MOS is written on the slate) it means that the scene will be shot without sound. The origin of the term is disputed. Some believe MOS stands for "motor only sound," and is a throwback to the days when special motors were needed to sync up picture and sound. The favored explanation is that when a German-born director, possibly Ernst Lubitsch or Fritz Lang, tried to announce that a scene would be shot "without sound," he said, in his accent, "this vun vee do mitout sound." "Mitout sound" became MOS. Regardless of origin, MOS today stands for "without sound."

motion artifact   Also called "strobing" or "Nyquist limit," this visual interference pattern has to do with the difference between a shot's frame rate and the motion of filmed objects. A common example would be a wheel that appears to be turning in the wrong direction.

Motion Picture Association of America (MPAA)   Formerly called the Motion Picture Producers and Distributors of America (MPPDA), this nonprofit association is considered the "voice" of the motion picture industry. It supports the interests of the movie studios (the current campaign against piracy, for example) and it administers the voluntary MPAA film rating system.

Motion Picture Editors Guild   A union for picture and sound editors, re-recording mixers, projectionists, recordists, boom operators, engineers, and story analysts.

Motion Picture Patents Company (MPPC)   Also known as the "Edison Trust" the MPPC was formed in 1908 by the major American film companies of the time in an effort to create a monopoly.

Motion Picture Producers and Distributers of America   Also called the "Hays Office," this was the film industry's method of self censorship created in 1922. *See* MPAA.

Motion Picture Sound Editors (MPSE)   An international professional association of sound editors, music editors, and sound designers. It is not a union. It has programs to mentor and educate young professionals and to make the community more aware of the advances in music and sound.

movematch   Also called "matchmove," "matchmoving," and "camera tracking." Refers to the use of computer programs to combine live footage and CGI effects.

multimedia artist   *See* animator.

music editor   Liaises between the composer and the director to ensure that music is used to accentuate and complement the live action, not overpower it. The music editor may create the sound track from a combination of an original score composed for the movie as well as the purchase of other music. The music editor uses a special computer software program to lay down the music tracks in sync with the picture.

National Association of Theatre Owners (NATO)   An exhibition trade organization representing over 29,000 movie theaters in the United States—including large chains and independent cinemas—and additional cinemas in 50 countries. It works to influence federal policy making that may impact cinemas, and it collaborates with distributors to address issues of joint concern, such as new technologies.

new deal   Changing set up for a new scene or a different camera position.

NG   No good.

Nickelodeon   The first theater devoted exclusively to showing films, opened in Pittsburgh in 1905. Prior to this, films were shown in conjunction with other events. Soon after the first one opened, nickelodeons sprung up all over the country.

nonlinear editing   Computer editing that does not necessitate editing in sequence.

notes   Comments on an idea or script, which may suggest changes.

NTSC   The U.S. and Canadian standard for TV and video display. It differs from PAL, the U.K. standard, and SECAM, the European standard.

nut   Operating expenses to be recovered.

off book   When an actor has memorized lines and no longer requires a script.

off-line   A preliminary edit done at lower cost to prepare an edit list for the more expensive on-line edit.

one hundred and eighty degree rule (180 degree rule)   If two people are filmed in sequence, the camera should not cross a line between them. The camera may be positioned anywhere within 180 degrees on one side of the line. Crossing the line results in a picture jump where the two people appear to have switched places.

on-line   The process of final editing.

option   When a producer, production company or studio purchases rights to a script for a limited amount of time. At the end of this time the studio or production company will either purchase the script outright or the rights will revert back to the writer, who is then free to try to sell the script elsewhere.

Oscar   The Academy Awards statue. Term coined by an unknown person who commented that the statue looked like his Uncle Oscar.

outtakes   Footage shot but not used in the final master.

over the shoulder shot   This shot is from the point of view of one character looking at another. The camera is placed behind (over the shoulder of) one person as it records the other person. Used when filming conversation.

ozoner   Slang for a drive-in theater.

package   The materials put together by the producer to usher the project through the development phase. These are the materials the studio will need to decide whether to accept or reject the proposal. The package usually contains a synopsis or treatment of the story idea, a marketing plan, production schedule, budget, artwork, cast or director commitments, and bios of key people involved.

pan　A camera shot in which the camera is slowly moved from left to right.

parallel editing　Cutting back and forth between two simultaneous scenes or stories.

pass　Rejection of a script from a studio, production company or agent. "Pass" may also refer to rewrites, such as the second "pass" of this script.

passion projects　Projects with limited marketability but with great personal meaning to the writer or producer.

pick up　When the director calls for a "pick up" it is to redo a small part of a scene. For example, if an actor flubbed one line, the director may redo or pick up just that line on another shot. In these cases, the pick up shot will have to be at a different angle than the previous shot or else there will be a jump cut. Thus if the director was shooting a long shot of a person, the pick up shot will be a medium or close up. The term "pick up" may also be used when referring a movie that was produced at one studio and acquired by another or by footage shot after the wrap.

piracy　Theft of a copyright motion picture.

pitch　Verbal description of a story idea or script. In a pitch meeting with a studio, a writer or producer may have only minutes to

Keeping in Touch

Decoding

It seems that filmmaking has more jargon than most other fields, possibly because things happen too fast on the set to use longer terms—and possibly because making up jargon is a fun distraction during a long shoot day. If the crew members purposefully confuse you in an effort to laugh at your inexperience, try to laugh with them. It is not personal. It is similar to a fraternity initiation. That said, if you can avoid wearing your inexperience on your sleeve, all the better. Study the words in this glossary, particularly the ones that pertain to your area. When you hear something unfamiliar on the set, remember it and check it out. If it is not listed here, call your mentor or a trusted friend, who will laugh with you, not at you.

pitch the idea and generate enough interest to move the project into development.

point of view (POV)   The character from whose perspective the scene is shot. If the camera is behind character A while filming character B, the shot is from A's point of view. Reaction shots are usually needed to establish point of view. POV shots can be done from a variety of perspectives. For example, you can shoot from an unidentified place in the room or from the POV of birds flying overhead.

polish   Final changes a writer makes to a script to get it ready for production.

postproduction   After the film is shot and graphics are created, the editors and sound staff put the film together.

postproduction supervisor   Coordinates all visual and audio aspects of the edit; maintains schedule and budget.

preproduction   The phase of production that begins when the green light is given to a script in development and ends when filming begins. It is everything that needs to be done in order to begin filming and to have filming go smoothly. During the preproduction phase, most of the key players are hired, filming arrangements are made, and sets are created.

prequel   A movie showing the characters in one movie at an earlier time, in another movie.

principal photography   The first day of shooting a movie.

print   A projectable version of the movie.

print it   When the director is satisfied with a particular scene and does not want to do it again, he or she yells "print it." A film print is then made of that take.

producer   The CEO of a film, the producer shepherds the idea through development, obtains financing, and oversees the entire production making sure it comes in on time and on budget.

Producers Guild of America (PGA)   A professional association for producers, including line producers, associate producers, assistant producers, unit production managers, producers, and executive producers.

production   Basically, this is part of the filmmaking process that involves the shooting of the film.

production assistant   Also known as a PA, this entry level position varies from set to set but usually includes running errands, getting catering, calling truckers, and other tasks. Sometimes a production assistant is assigned to a major director or actor as a one-on-one assistant during a production.

production coordinator   Coordinates logistics, ships film, gets dailies, arranges transportation and accommodations, and deals with emergencies.

production designer   The production designer is responsible for the physical look of the film and therefore works closely with the director and the director of photography. The production designer oversees everyone who contributes to the physical appearance, including set designers and decorators, costume designers, and hair and makeup artists.

production report   A daily report of what was actually shot compared to what had been planned on the production schedule.

production schedule   A plan of what will be filmed each day.

production sound mixer   *See* sound engineer.

product placement   This is when a recognizable product is used in a movie in exchange for some type of benefit to the movie. The benefit may be free product or funding for the film. When cars are used in chase and crash scenes, the donated cars represent a considerable saved expense for the producer. Cereal boxes and candy wrappers do not in themselves offer any financial benefit, and in those cases the manufacturer provides funding.

project slate   All the scripts a particular CE or DE has in development.

promotion manager or unit publicist   The promotional aspect of marketing a film focuses on arranging interviews with stars and the director and placing stories about the upcoming film in print and broadcast media.

prompter   A person out of view who gives actors lines if they forget.

property   A script, book or other literary material.

prop master   Reviews the script and makes a list of props that will be needed. The prop master obtains the props and maintains them in good condition, making sure they are ready when needed.

purchase contract   An agreement between a writer and a studio or production company for a script written on spec. The purchase contract outlines what the company will pay for all rights along with additional payments if the property is produced.

pyrotechnician   Someone with expertise in creating explosions or fires.

quartz light   Also called a "halogen light" or a "tungsten," this is a very bright light.

query   A letter from a writer to a producer or agent that briefly describes the story idea. This is usually the first step before developing a treatment or script.

rack focus   Changing camera focus while shooting.

ratings system   In 1968, Jack Valenti of the Motion Pictures Association of America (MPAA) replaced the Hayes Office guidelines with a rating system, similar to the one used today.

reaction shot   When you are shooting from one actor's point of view, you usually shoot reaction shots of the person to whom he is speaking.

reflective light reading   Measurement of the amount of light bouncing off a subject; obtained with a light meter.

registration   Refers to camera and degree to which one frame lines up with the next.

re-recording mixer   In post, the sound re-recording mixer mixes all the audio elements, such as dialogue, music, and special effects.

reverse angle   When you move the camera to show the set from the opposite side. This is helpful in establishing a point-of-view (POV) shot. Reverse angle shots or reverse shots are often used to film a conversation from the point of view of each character.

rigger   The person who hangs lights and puts up scaffolding.

room tone   Before striking the set in a location, the sound recordist will record a few minutes of tape when no one is speaking. This ambient sound, or room tone, may be used in editing to make a studio recording sound like it was recorded on the set. Everyone is quiet and stays in place on the set while room tone is being recorded.

rough cut   An edited version of the film done prior to the final edit. The rough cut may not have all the effects. It is used to see if the general sequence is effective.

rushes   Work print returned from the lab.

sabre artist   Uses a combination of software programs to create visual effects.

safety   While filming, this is a shot done after an acceptable shot. It is backup.

scene   A part of the movie that is shot in one location and represents one block of time.

Screen Actors Guild (SAG)   The main union for actors.

screen test   An on-camera audition.

script colors   Each time a script is revised it is printed on a different color paper to help people keep track and know the most up to date version. The colors, in order, are: white, blue, pink, yellow, green, gold, buff, salmon, cherry, tan, back to white.

script consultant   Someone a writer pays to review a script before submitting it to an agent or producer. The script consultant is someone knowledgeable about the industry who will give the writer specific feedback on how to make the script more appealing to a studio.

script reader   The script reader is hired by the studio, usually on a freelance basis, to review scripts submitted to the studio. The script reader is the first person to review the script and attaches a report recommending that the creative execs read the script, suggesting that it be "considered," or advising that the studio "pass." *See* coverage.

script supervisor   On the set the script supervisor follows the script and marks how each take of each scene was shot. Was it good or were there flubs? Was it a close up or a wide shot? This information helps the editor.

set   The environment used for filming. You can film in one location—the library, for example—but with different sets, such as the check-out counter, the stacks, and a table for reading.

set decorator   Decorates the set similarly to the way an interior decorator decorates your home. The set decorator chooses furnishing, fabrics, and other items that reflect the overall design established by the production designer.

set designer   Adapts the production designer's vision into blueprints that can be followed by everyone involved in creating the set. The set designer supervises the construction crew, carpenters, painters, and other craftspeople.

set up   This refers to adjusting the camera and lights to change the shot, either because the scene is to be redone from a different angle or you are moving on to another scene.

shooting ratio   The amount of film shot compared to the amount used. Can refer to the usable footage of a day, but more often refers to the total amount shot compared to the running time of the film. For instance, if you shoot 30 minutes of film to produce a finished 5 minute program, your shooting ratio is 6:1.

shot list   The production crew receives this list at the start of each day. It provides the scene number and location of each scene scheduled for that day. It also describes everything that will be needed for each scene, such as actors and props.

sides A small section of a script, usually one to 10 pages, given to an actor at an audition. The actor is given a short time to look over the lines before auditioning. Sides may also refer to the section of script that will be shot on a particular day and which is distributed to cast and crew at the beginning of the shooting day.

signatory A studio or production company that is an official member of the Screen Actors Guild (SAG) or the Writers Guild of America (WGA).

silk A large piece of filmy white cloth used to filter light.

slate (1) If you are an actor at an audition and you are asked to "slate," you should look directly into the camera lens and state your name, and, if applicable, the name of the agency that represents you. Begin your monologue as soon as you have done this. (2) If you are on the set, a black board with two hinges (clapboard) will be photographed before each shot. The slate will show the scene number, take, and whether it is being shot with sync sound or MOS.

slug line In a script the location, date, and time the action is supposed to be in is listed above each scene.

Society of Motion Picture and Television Engineers (SMPTE) This technical society outlines measurements and standards of the industry.

Society of Operating Cameramen (SOC) This organization is composed of outstanding camera operators from around the world.

soft light A light with a built in surface to act as a bounce card, thereby providing soft, indirect light. May also refer to a new type of wireless lighting controlled by computer.

solicited A script that the producer or studio requests from a writer. Generally, if the producer likes a query he or she will solicit a script.

sound blanket The same as the quilted blanket used by movers, the sound blanket is put up to block out sound from another room (on location).

sound designer During postproduction, the sound designer (also known as the sound effects editor or special effects editor) identifies where special sound effects are needed—such as a gunshot, dog barking, or door closing—and produces those effects.

sound mixer The sound mixer, also known as the production sound mixer—or better known as the "sound man"—is responsible to the director for the quality of sound recorded for each scene.

sound stage A large indoor area for filming where lighting, sound, temperature, and other variables can be controlled.

spec A script written with the hope (on speculation) that it might sell.

special effects These are effects created optically, with the camera, or mechanically by manipulating items on the set. This is in contrast to visual effects which are created on the computer.

speed On the set, "speed" means the camera is rolling, sound is being recorded, and that the sound is up to speed or in sync with camera. When the crew announces "speed," it mean the director can begin shooting. "Action" will closely follow "speed."

splice Today most editing is done digitally. But when film is edited, it is spliced together. *Splice* refers to a way of attaching one piece of film to another.

spotting session At the beginning of postproduction, the director meets with members of the sound team to discuss the various components of sounds and to make sure there is a coordinated effect.

squib A small device that simulates the sound of a gun shot or small explosion. When worn by an actor, a squib includes a container of simulated blood that will burst when it is punctured.

stand-in Someone who is about the same height and coloring as an actor stands in the actor's place while lights are adjusted.

steadicam A camera attached to the camera operator with a mechanical harness to steady it when the operator moves.

stock footage Stored footage from other productions that can be inserted in a movie to save filming costs. For example, a crowd scene may be picked up from another film.

storyboard A scene-by-scene visualization of the film.

streaming A type of IPTV in which the film is transmitted in pieces to the hard drive and then destroyed.

supervising sound editor Makes sure that all facets of sound postproduction are on schedule and on budget. Often the same person functions as the sound designer and supervising sound editor.

swing gang Set dressers who set up and strike sets before or after the production crew appears.

synopsis A one-half to two-page description of a story.

take A scene that is being, or has been, filmed. Each time a scene is redone it is a different "take." (For example, you will hear, "Scene 1, take 2.") A script supervisor makes a note of each take, to help the editor choose shots in post. The director may call for another take to improve upon the way something was done in the scene or to do the scene from another angle. Although the editor will look at several takes to choose the best ones, he or she can ignore the takes where there were problems, such as flubbed lines. The editor may want to cut together a take done as a wide shot with a take done as a close up of a particular character.

tent pole film   This is a high-budget film viewed by the studio as a potential blockbuster. The term *tent pole* comes from the image of this film holding up the tent of the studio.

terra-filte   A cross between a steadicam and a louma crane used to steady images.

tie-in kit   Device used to bypass the fuse box and electrical wiring at a location and tap directly into power from the mains.

time code   Electronic code to reference footage for editing.

track   To follow a project through development.

trades   The "trade papers" are daily show biz periodicals. The most popular ones are the *Hollywood Reporter* and *Variety.*

traveling matte shot   *See* blue screen *and* green screen.

treatment   A summary of a script, but much longer and in more depth than a synopsis. The treatment provides a scene-by-scene description of the story and may run anywhere from a few pages to over 30 pages.

turnaround   After a designated period of time (the turnaround) a studio or production company will offer a script that it has not yet produced to outside buyers. The outside buyer usually has to reimburse the studio for any costs it incurred.

two-shot   Shot of two characters usually done as a medium close-up, from the chest up.

undercranking   When the camera frame rate is slowed so the action seems to be in fast motion.

unit production manager   Protects the producer's financial interests by monitoring the budget and schedule and trying to get the most cost-effective deals with companies or freelancers helping with the production. The unit production manager works closely with the production accountant, tracks expenditures, and pays bills.

unit publicist   Member of publicity department who follows the crew and cast on location and tries to set up interviews for the cast.

unsolicited   Refers to a script submitted to a producer, agent, studio, or anyone who didn't request one by that person or company.

Solicited scripts (requested after a query letter or verbal pitch) are reviewed more quickly than unsolicited scripts.

vertical integration   This is when a media company purchases a company in another part of the process. For example, if a media company owns a production company and it purchases a distribution company, this is vertical integration.

vertigo effect   Hitchcock created this camera technique while filming *Vertigo*. The camera tracks backwards while zooming in and gives the impression that the character being filmed is stationary while his or her surroundings change.

visual effects   These effects are created on the computer, in contrast to special effects, which are created optically or mechanically.

voice   The way in which the writer's unique style or point of view comes through the script, making it somewhat unique and more interesting.

voice-over   Dialogue that will be used in the sound track while another image appears on the screen.

walla   Also known as "rhubarb" because in the past extras in a crowd would be asked to mumble the word "rhubarb" to simulate background conversation.

whip pan   A very fast camera pan that causes motion blur.

wild sound   Sound recorded without picture.

Wilhelm scream   A distinctive scream, first recorded during the filming of *Distant Drums* in 1951, this scream was archived by Warner Bros. and has been re-used many times.

wipe   An editing transition where a border rolls across the scene as one scene transitions to another.

work for hire   An employment contract in which a the employer maintains copyright of the script.

working title   What the movie is called during production. The title used during filming may not be the title when the film is released.

wrap   Director calls "That's a wrap," to let everyone know that filming is over for the day.

Writers Guild of America (WGA)   This is the union for screenwriters.

Chapter 6

Resources

This chapter provides resources for both the "need to know" and the "nice to know." There are listings for job sources, training courses, and unions. Periodicals to help you stay current with what is going on in the film industry, including technology, are listed. Some of the books described offer practical information you can use on the job, and other books give a glimpse into the more human side of the industry. Several of the associations and organizations listed below function as labor unions, offer educational seminars, and provide networking opportunities.

Associations and Organizations

Academy of Motion Picture Arts and Sciences is an honorary membership organization with over 6,000 artists and professionals. In addition to being in charge of the famed Oscars, the Academy sponsors numerous screenings, events, and exhibitions throughout the year and may offer good opportunities for networking. (http://www.oscars.org)

Actors' Equity is a union representing over 48,000 American actors and stage managers working in live theater. (http://www.actorsequity.org)

American Federation of Television and Radio Actors (AFTRA) is a national labor union representing over 70,000 performers, journalists, and others working in the entertainment or news media. (http://www.aftra.com)

American Society of Cinematographers (ASC) is an elite non-profit association with membership by invitation only. Members are chosen based on their body of work, and there are only 302 members from 20 countries. But this organization can be very helpful to young filmmakers. ASC members volunteer their time to provide educational programs and mentorship to aspiring filmmakers. The organization publishes a magazine and a manual (see the "Books and Periodicals" subsection of this chapter). Books may also be purchased online through its Web site. (http://www.ascmag.com)

Art Directors Guild and Scenic, Title, and Graphic Artists is a local union of the International Alliance of Theatrical and Stage Employees (IATSE). It represents 104,000 members including art directors, graphic artists, illustrators, set designers, scenic artists, model makers, illustrators, matte artist, digital artists, and title artists. (http://www.artdirectors.org)

Association of Film Commissioners International (AFCI) offers information about what they will offer in terms of tax incentives, grants, interest free loans, and other programs to facilitate filming. (http://www.afci.org)

Directors Guild of America (DGA) is a union and professional association that protects directors' legal and artistic rights. It has a mentorship committee to assist new directors and it has committees focusing on diversity and on women. It publishes a magazine, the *DGA Quarterly*. The DGA provides health and pension plans for members. To date there are 14,000 members comprising directors, first and second assistant directors, unit production managers, tape associate directors, stage managers, and production associates. (http://www.dga.org)

Federation Internationale des Association de Producteurs de Films (FIAPF) is known in the United States as The International Federation of Film Producers Association. It represents 25 producer organizations from 22 countries, including the Motion Picture Association and the Independent Film and TV Alliance. This is not an organization joined by individuals, but it also regulates international film festivals. (http://www.fiapf.org)

Film Society of Lincoln Center seeks to recognize and support new filmmakers. It premieres new films from established and emerging directors, provides retrospectives, and offers in-depth symposia. (http://www.filmlinc.com)

IFP.org is set up to support the independent filmmaker. Since its inception in 1979, IFP has supported the production of 7,000 films and provided resources to over 20,000 filmmakers. IFP represents approximately 10,000 filmmakers around the world and offers workshops, seminars, conferences, and mentorships. It also publishes *Filmmaker Magazine*. IFP seeks to build audiences for independent films by hosting screenings in conjunction with other cultural events. IFP's annual script-to-screen conference is an opportunity for independent filmmakers to learn from and connect with decision makers in the business. (http://www.ifp .org)

International Alliance of Theatrical and Stage Employees (IATSE) represents technicians, artisans, and craftspeople in the entertainment industry, including those in motion pictures, television, theater, and trade. (http:// www.iatse-intl.org)

International Animated Film Society is a nonprofit organization that sponsors screenings and educational seminars and preserves films in danger of being lost. (http://www.asifa-hollywood.org)

International Cinematographers Guild (ICG) is the union for cinematographers, IATSE 600. One of the best features of the Web site is a review of all the latest technology. Go to the left column on the home page and click "tech tips." Press "links" in that

Problem Solving

Need Money, No Work

If you are working in production: Since most jobs in the film industry are on a project-by-project basis, it is not uncommon to have days with no income. This is a time to think outside of the box. If you have word processing or other computer skills, check the yellow pages in your town and sign up with temp agencies. Once you are known to an agency they will begin to call you more regularly when someone needs a temp.

If you are looking for an assistant job at a studio or production company: Call the temp agencies to find out which ones have contracts with the different studios. Sign up with those agencies. This is a good way to make contacts and to support yourself while you look for a full-time job.

column, then click "sites with job listings," and you will find a list of 11 Web sites featuring a variety of types of jobs in the entertainment industry. The ICG publishes the monthly magazine, *ICG Magazine*. (http://www.cameraguild.com)

International Documentary Association (IDA) is a professional association for documentary filmmakers. IDA publishes the journal *Documentary* and sponsors a variety of events of interest to documentary filmmakers. (http://www.documentary.org)

Motion Picture Association of America (MPAA) is the voice and advocate for the American motion picture, video, and television industries. It is aligned with the Motion Picture Association (MPA), which is international. The MPAA rates movies in conjunction with the National Association of Theater owners, performs research, and provides educational outreach. Right now it is most actively focused on fighting piracy and protecting copyright. (http://www.mpaa.org)

Motion Picture Editors Guild is open to all postproduction professionals, including those in sound. The union publishes *Editor's Guild*, a magazine. (http://www.editorsguild.com)

Producers Guild of America (PGA) is a professional association, not a union. Membership provides excellent educational and networking opportunities through educational seminars, mentoring programs, and admission to special screenings, including those associated with the Academy Awards. There is also a members only job board and a newsletter, *PGA Produced By*. Members may participate in the Motion Picture Industry Pension and Health Plan. Membership requirements vary depending on the medium, so it is best to contact the PGA directly to assess your qualifications. The association is set up to support producers, "those on the career path to becoming producers," and other team members. (http://www.producersguild.org)

Screen Actors Guild (SAG) is primarily a union, and an excellent one, but it also offers many of the benefits of a professional association, such as educational events and a quarterly publication, *Screen Actor*. As a union, however, is where SAG shines. All studios and many major production companies hire only SAG actors, and the union has set strict guidelines regarding pay and working conditions for its members. SAG negotiates contracts, helps actors recoup unpaid residuals, offers group health insurance, and provides many other services to its 120,000 members.

There are many local chapters across the country. The Web site also carries a list of SAG franchised agents. To be eligible for membership, an actor must work three days of background or one day as a principal performer on a SAG production and must be paid the union rate. (http://www.sag.org)

Writers Guild of America (WGA) is a union and professional association with over 9,500 members provides a wide range of services. A highlight of the site is WGAWRegistry.org, which is available to members and nonmembers. This is an easy way to protect yourself by registering your script before you send it to anyone, including an agent, manager, or producer. In addition to union functions, WGA offers health insurance and many educational seminars, special events, and publications. WGA publishes the magazine *Written By.* (http://wga.org)

Books and Periodicals

Books

Beyond the Red Carpet: Keys to Becoming a Successful Personal Assistant. By Dionne M. Muhammad (Authorhouse, 2006). Whether you see a personal assistant job at the studio, in a production company, or for a high-level producer or director as a stepping stone or a career in itself, this book can help you break in and achieve success in your role. It is written as "continuing education" for those working as personal assistants as well as a guide for those trying to break in. Today's PAs need to understand the commercial side of the business, have public relations and communication skills, and be solid project managers.

Breakfast with Sharks: A Screenwriter's Guide to Getting the Meeting, Nailing the Pitch, Signing the Deal, and Navigating the Murky Waters of Hollywood. By Michael Lent (Three Rivers Press, 2004). Do not be put off by this book's 2004 release date. Some of the phone numbers and Web sites listed may have changed, but the solid, practical information provided has not. An entertaining writer, Lent shares his personal experiences as he guides readers through every stage of the process from whether or not you should move to Los Angeles, to how to keep your personal voice but make your work marketable, to how to deal with producers, studio executives, and directors. There is practical information on how to manage your life, such as where to find temp jobs, and inside information on what it really means when someone says they will "consider" your script. This is not a how to write a script book. Its focus is how to make your script marketable and how to sell it. In that vein, Lent decodes studio and producer-speak and shares his insights on how to deal with everyone in the industry.

The Complete Film Production Handbook **(3rd edition).** By Eve Light Honthaner (Focal Press, 2001). This step by step guide to preproduction, production, and postproduction includes checklists, schedules, contracts, information about insurance, and talent management. Sample forms for working with SAG, DGA, WGA, production forms, deal memos, and release forms are there as well. Experienced producers and production managers will find this book to be a handy reference. Production assistants will find that it acquaints them with the day-to-day procedures.

God, Man, and Hollywood: Politically Incorrect Cinema from The Birth of a Nation to The Passion of Christ. By Mark Royden Winchell (ISI Books, 2008). Although this book itself may be politically incorrect, the insights it gives into some controversial films—insights with which you may not agree—are thought provoking.

Gods and Monsters. By Peter Biskind (Nation Books, 2004). This book is a compilation of over 30 years of Biskind's articles from a variety of publications. It is a well-written, inside-scoop type of book by an engaging writer.

Hollywood Undercover: Revealing the Sordid Secrets of Tinseltown. By Ian Halperin (Mainstream Publishing Company, 2007). An entertaining, gossipy exposé.

The Mailroom: Hollywood History from the Bottom Up. By David Rensin (Ballantine Books, 2003). Rensin offers a funny, entertaining, insightful history of superstars—including David Geffen, Barry Diller, and Michael Ovitz—who started their careers in the mailrooms of major Hollywood agencies.

Producing for Hollywood: A Guide for Independent Producers **(2nd edition).** By Paul Mason and Don Gold (Allworth Press, 2004). When this book was released, Leonard B. Stern, chairman of the Advisory Council of the Producers Guild of America (PGA), wrote, "If you have only time to read one book on what you need to know to succeed as a producer and filmmaker, read Paul Mason and Donald Gold's *Producing for Hollywood.*" This book is a roadmap for aspiring producers with step by step guidance about how to put together a package and how to obtain financing. There are invaluable insights that can come only from industry pros, such as how to read a script. Since moviemaking is a group deal even if you are an independent filmmaker, there are chapters are dealing with writers and actors. There are six appendices you will photocopy and use often, including an example of a film partnership proposal, contact information for foreign distributors,

The Sundance Kids: How the Mavericks Took Back Hollywood. By James Mottram (Faber and Faber, 2006). An engrossing read about independent filmmakers getting Hollywood studios to produce their non-mainstream films. A fascinating, uplifting book.

This Business of Film: A Practical Guide to Achieving Success in the Film Industry. By Stephen R. Greenwald and Paula Landry (Lone Eagle, 2009). You undoubtedly have many books on film in your library and probably try to keep yourself from buying one more. But this book is a must have for anyone in any part of the industry—corporate, production, or writing. The text of the book provides an in-depth view of how every part of the industry functions. It has organizational charts, which clearly reveal reporting lines. For potential producers, there

Keeping in Touch

The Associations

As you read the list of associations, guilds, and organizations in this chapter, do not focus only on whether or not you meet the qualifications for membership. In fact, do not limit yourself to your area of work. Most of these organizations have screenings, seminars, and informal get-togethers, usually arranged through the local chapter. This can be a good way to make contacts in the industry and perhaps find a mentor. If you are considering taking an additional course or training program, speak with someone at the organization to determine which programs are reputable.

is a wealth of information about how to put together a package for a studio or investor, how to obtain financing, how to create a budget, and how to deal with writers. Writers will find information on script formatting and copyrighting. Extensive information on distribution, exhibition, and marketing is included. Accountants and lawyers will get a good sense of the legal and financial details of the film industry.

The Whole Equation: A History of Hollywood. By David Thomson (Knopf, 2004). This Hollywood history book has a different slant and includes a lot of information not known to the general public. A bedtime read.

The X List: The National Society of Film Critics' Guide to the Movies That Turn Us On. Edited by Jami Bernard (De Capo Press, 2005). Good bedtime reading to relax after a hard day on the set. This book includes critiques by several noted film critics of some of the movies that turned them on most. Eighty films are critiqued including: *The Age of Innocence, Basic Instinct, Butch Cassidy and the Sundance Kid, Blue Velvet, Deep Throat, The Fabulous Baker Boys, McCabe and Mrs. Miller, Wuthering Heights,* and *Young Lady Chatterley.*

Writing from the Inside Out; Transforming Your Psychological Blocks to Release the Writer Within. By Dennis Palumbo (John Wiley and Sons, 2000). A successful screenwriter, whose credits include *My Favorite Year* and *Welcome Back Kotter,* Palumbo became a licensed psychotherapist focusing largely on helping writers overcome their blocks to writing. He addresses the internal struggles faced by writers. This book is recommended by both seasoned and aspiring writers.

Periodicals

American Cinematographer is a prestigious international journal published by the American Society of Cinematographers. The ASC also publishes a manual for cinematographers and students. (http://www.ascmag.com)

Backstage is an excellent resource for actors, this newspaper includes job listings, a directory of acting classes, photographers and others sources used by actors. As a publication, there are news and feature stories, movie reviews, and advice columns (focused on tips for actors). (http://www.backstage.com)

Creative Screenwriting lets writers know which genres are popular (have the best chance of selling at the moment), which agencies are looking for clients, and which producers are looking for scripts. It includes interviews with top writers. Regular columns include Ron Suppa on the business of screenwriting, Karl Iglesias with advice on the craft of writing, and interviews with agents. (http://www.creativescreenwriting.com)

Fade In is a new magazine that covers industry news, current movies, and so on. It keeps you up-to-date on what is going on around town (if your town is Hollywood or New York). (http://www.fadeinonline.com)

Filmmaker is published by the IFP and is available for digital or mail subscription. A newsletter is also published. The magazine is geared to independent filmmakers but has articles of interest to others. (http://www.filmmakermagazne.com)

Hollywood Reporter is a daily publication that helps you stay current on industry news in film, television and technology. (http://www.hollywoodreporter.com)

ICG Magazine is a monthly magazine published by the International Cinematographers Guild. (http://www.icgmagazine.com)

MovieMaker is a bimonthly magazine about the art and business of making movies. It includes criticism, profiles of key industry figures, and festival coverage. (http://www.moviemaker.com)

Script Magazine has been providing writers with articles on the craft of writing as well as the marketing of screenplays for 11 years. Most articles in the bimonthly magazine are written by screenwriters and development executives. (http://www.scriptmag.com)

Variety is a daily newspaper focuses on the business of entertainment. (http://www.variety.com)

Other Media

Films

The following four films deal with filmmaking in very different ways. Frank Prinzi, ASC, who is interviewed in Chapter 4, was cinematographer for *Living in Oblivion*. If you have not seen these films, head straight for Netflix, Blockbuster, or the library.

Contempt (Le Mepris). This 1963 film by Jean Luc Godard deals with the perennial conflict between film as art and film for commercial opportunity as it portrays a director (Fritz Lang, playing himself) trying to make a film version of Homer's *Odyssey*. The film starts Brigitte Bardot and Jack Palance.

Day for Night (La Nuit Americaine). A 1973 film by Francois Truffaut, portrays a "film within a film" and centers on the characters involved in making the film. The film's director, Ferrand, played by Truffaut, is seen grappling with the many problems a director faces during production of a movie. *Day for Night* won the Academy Award for Best Foreign Language Film and is considered to be one of Truffaut's greatest films.

Get Shorty. This 1995 comedy by Barry Sonnenfeld, based on the novel by Elmore Leonard, follows a mobster as he goes to Hollywood to collect a debt. Once there he learns that his mobster skills suit him well when he becomes a producer. The film won a Golden Globe Award.

Living in Oblivion. This 1994 independent feature by Tom DiCillo is another film within a film, but far less glamorous than *Day for Night*. The characters trying to make a movie here are humorously incompetent, egotistical, or both.

DVDs

The Action/Cut Filmmaking DVD Pro Collection is a condensed version of director/writer Guy Magar's two-day seminar. This 12-hour, 3 DVD collection includes schedules and budgets, camera shot lists, visual effects, and financing. A workbook is included.

Hollywood Camera Work: The Master Course in High-End Blocking and Staging is a nine-hour 3D animated course includes six DVDs. It is geared primarily to directors and cinematographers, but may be of interest to other members of the production and postproduction team. The course focuses on single-camera blocking and is designed to help directors do the most effective blocking with the best production value.

Independent Filmmaking Using Gorilla is a two-and-a-half hour tutorial reviews how to breakdown a script for shooting, enter elements, link elements together, schedule cast and crew and track expenses. There are more elaborate, more expensive, Gorilla DVDs with more information and a means to track projects.

Truby's Great Screenwriting Class DVD is screenwriter John Truby's eight-hour course that has been used by many successful screenwriters and has won numerous awards. It is presented in this DVD, which includes 22 building blocks of every great script, three variations to classic structure, seven steps to a great premise, four requirements for a good hero, five major character changes, and how to write three-track dialogue.

Web Sites

Many of the Web sites described below feature job listings and/or training programs. This section also includes a guide to film festivals and screenwriting contests.

Career Development

These resources offer tools pf the trade to those in the industry. They also offer network opportunities.

American Film Institute offers a graduate film school program and hands-on courses in varying parts of the business. The courses generally require a full time commitment, so you are unable to work while taking a course. But this is something to consider if you have been in the business awhile and now know exactly what you want to do. For example, do you love editing? The AFI editing course is a two-year program done in a postproduction facility that includes 15 Avid Symphony bays and one AVID Nitris networked through the AVID Unity media storage system. If you are a woman interested in directing, AFI has a course geared specifically for women. Alumnae include Leslie Linka Glatter (*Heroes, The Closer*), Randa Haines (*Children of a Lesser God*), and many other successful women directors. (http://www.afi.com)

Atlantic Television provides local crews across the country to those filming on location. (http://www.atlantictv.com)

Central Casting can work for you, whether you are pursuing a career in acting or just trying to earn some money while you follow your dream for a job in another segment of the industry. This agency places background actors and has offices in Los Angeles and New York. (http://www.centralcasting.org)

EntertainmentCareers.Net lists a wide range of production or production-related jobs from all over the country—director, assistant director, field producer, audio engineer, payroll accountant, audience coordinator assistant, and more. Also lists hundred of internships. (http://www.entertainmentcareers.net)

The Film School Directory provides a list of film schools and training programs by state as well background information on the industry. (http://www.filmschools.com)

Film Staff provides job listings for animators, editors, gaffers, grips—pretty much any position in film. (http://www.filmstaff .com)

Hollywood Film Institute is a superb Web site for educational programs and resources. The HFI offers a long list of two-day on-site programs, on-line courses, and DVDs. All programs are specifically targeted an area of interest, such as editing, screenwriting, budgeting, and scheduling a production. Classes are hands-on and designed to simulate a real work environment. If you click on "resources" at the top, you will find a list of excellent links for everything from buying equipment to finding film commissions. Click on film commissions on the left and a list will appear on the right. You can then click to be connected to the film commission of your choice. (http://www .hollywoodu.com)

IMDb, The Internet Movie Database is great for up-to-date information about movies and lots of box office stats. IMDb pro, available as a paid subscription, is an amazing resource with contact listings for talent, companies, agents, and pretty much anyone you would want to reach. Through pro you also get news from the *Hollywood Reporter*, which might save you the cost of an additional subscription. There is also a résumé service offered. (http://www.imdb.com)

Interactives: Cinema offers background information on the film industry and careers. It includes lists of different types of courses, including online courses and workshops. (http://www.learner .org/interactives/cinema)

Showbizjobs.com lists jobs that deal primarily with the business end of film, such as production accountants, attorneys, and so. Some production-related jobs are also posted. (http://www .showbizjobs.com)

On the Cutting Edge

Periodicals and Seminars

The technological end of filmmaking changes so fast it is difficult for anyone to keep up. Take a look at the cinematography magazines and other periodicals that feature new technology. Look at Web sites that review tech developments. This is good for on-the-set conversation. Also check the "tech tips" on the ICG Web site.

Sun Oasis is a great site if you are looking for in-between-job temp work, this Web site lists freelance writing and editing jobs. This is a possible way to make between-job income for anyone with writing or editing skills, particularly aspiring screenwriters. (http://www.sunoasis.com)

Theatr Group is an educational site that features articles for actors and links to practical information an actor needs, such as head shots, classes, unions, and managers. There is résumé help as well. (http://www.theatrgroup.com)

Variety has a feature where can post your résumé on the Web site, which includes listings for both business and creative jobs nationwide and abroad. You can search job listings here as well. (http://www.variety.com)

Wikipedia has many interesting and useful articles about the film industry. (http://www.en.wikipedia.org)

Writers Store is not for writers only. It includes materials for filmmaking production as well. It is an easy-to-navigate site from which you can read industry magazine articles for free or purchase educational DVDs, books, and periodical subscriptions or sign up for on-line courses. (http://www.writersstore.com)

Festivals and Contests

Festivals and contests are a great way to get noticed and to make contacts, particularly if your work is well regarded. If you do well at a film festival there will probably be distributors right there anxious to meet you. If you do well in a screenwriting competition, noting so on a script can help it get past the reader and to the CE or DE.

Contests for Screenwriters includes a list of contests for screenwriters, and you can submit your script via the Web site. (http://www.filmmakers.com/contests)

4,000 Film Festivals lists and describes over 4,000 film festivals and you can submit and manage your entry on the site. It also includes job listings for the festivals. (http://www.fest21.com)

Guide to International Film Festivals is a guide to the 52 international film festivals accredited by the Federation Internationale des Associations de Producteurs de Films (FIAPF). The brochure offers information about the film categories shown at that festival (documentary, animation, full-length feature, and so on) the number of press and distributors in attendance, and all the logistical details. (http://www.fiapf.org/pdf/directoryFIAPFv3.pdf)

Nicholl Fellowships in Screenwriting awards up to five $30,000 fellowships annually to writers who have previously earned less than $5,000 writing for film or television. (http://www.oscars .org/awards/nicholl/index.html)

Without a Box takes the stress out of submitting your film to festivals. You can use it to submit to multiple festivals simultaneously and to promote and distribute your independent film. (http:// withoutabox.com)

Index

in Golden Age of Hollywood,
7–8
high concept, 117
low-concept, 120
manager, 78–79
passion projects, 124
target audience of, 42
Marley and Me, 46
Martini Shot, 109
Mason, Paul, 138–139
matte artist, 121
M&E. *See* music and effects
medium shot, 121
mentors, 67, 86–88
method acting, 121
Michigan, 45
Miramax Films, 20
mix, 121
modeler, 121
money, 135
MOS. *See* motor only sound
motion artifact, 121–122
Motion Picture Association
(MPA), 136
Motion Picture Association of
America (MPAA), 16, 42, 122,
127, 136
on employment, 43
Motion Picture Editors Guild, 122,
136
Motion Picture Patents Company
(MPPC), 3, 7, 122
Motion Picture Producers and
Distributors of America, 8, 16,
122
motion pictures. *See* films
Motion Picture Sound Editors
(MPSE), 122
motor only sound (MOS), 121
Mottram, James, 139
movematch, 122
MovieMaker, 141
movie making. *See* filmmaking
movies. *See* films

MPA. *See* Motion Picture
Association
MPAA. *See* Motion Picture
Association of America
MPPC. *See* Motion Picture Patents
Company
MPSE. *See* Motion Picture Sound
Editors
Muhammad, Dionne M., 137
multimedia artist. *See* animator/
visual effects artist
music and effects (M&E), 121
music editor, 74, 122
Muybridge, Eadweard, 2

N

NAACP. *See* National Association
for the Advancement of Colored
People
National Amusements, 31
National Association for the
Advancement of Colored People
(NAACP), 6
National Association of Theatre
Owners (NATO), 122
NATO. *See* National Association of
Theatre Owners
NBC, 31
networking, 67, 82–84, 139
new deal, 123
News Corporation, 31
New York City, 90
NG. *See* no good
Nicholl Fellowships in
Screenwriting, 145
Nickelodeon, 3, 123
Noci Pictures Entertainment, 44
no good (NG), 123
nonlinear editing, 123
non-theatrical production, 30
notes, 123
NTSC, 123
nudity, 16
nut (expenses), 123